Praise for *Socrates*

W9-BYM-559

"Johnson writes more concisely than most scholars and brings to his prose a wealth of anecdote and asides unknown to most academics. His Socrates comes alive not through arguments over Platonic dating or Pythagorean influence, but by wit and allusion to Jane Austen novels, Samuel Johnson, John Maynard Keynes, firsthand remembrances of Winston Churchill's speeches, and Richard Dawkins. A valuable overview."
—*The Washington Times*

"Spectacular . . . a delight to read." —*The Wall Street Journal*

"Robust." —*The New Republic*

"With effortless erudition, Paul Johnson brings to life the world of the great philosopher." —*Women's Wear Daily*

"This snappy biography goes down easy while offering a full portrait of Socrates—the man, the thinker, the celebrity—and the world he lived in." —*Zócalo Public Square*

"Delivered in his typically robust, confident manner, this work reconfirms Johnson as one of the most popular of popular historians." —*Booklist*

"[Johnson's] genuine love of the demos makes him an all-too-rare figure in today's chattering classes." —*First Things*

"Enlightening . . . Johnson disentangles centuries of scarce and questionable sources to offer a riveting account of a homely but charismatic middle-class man whose ideas still shape the way we decide how to act, and how we fathom the notion of body and soul." —*History Book Club*

"A wonderfully readable account of life in Athens, its political quarrels, and its failures. As good as a murder mystery, Johnson's narrative is exciting." —*Library Journal*

PENGUIN BOOKS

SOCRATES

Paul Johnson is an acclaimed historian of extraordinary range whose many bestselling books have been translated into dozens of languages. He has written for *The Spectator, Forbes, The Wall Street Journal,* and *The New York Times,* among many other publications. He is also the author of *Darwin: Portrait of a Genius,* available from Viking, and will publish his biography of Mozart in 2013. He lives in London.

PAUL JOHNSON

Socrates

A Man for Our Times

PENGUIN BOOKS

PENGUIN BOOKS
Published by the Penguin Group
Penguin Group (USA) Inc., 375 Hudson Street, New York, New York 10014, U.S.A.
Penguin Group (Canada), 90 Eglinton Avenue East, Suite 700, Toronto,
Ontario, Canada M4P 2Y3 (a division of Pearson Penguin Canada Inc.)
Penguin Books Ltd, 80 Strand, London WC2R 0RL, England
Penguin Ireland, 25 St. Stephen's Green, Dublin 2, Ireland (a division of Penguin Books Ltd)
Penguin Group (Australia), 707 Collins Street, Melbourne, Victoria 3008, Australia
(a division of Pearson Australia Group Pty Ltd)
Penguin Books India Pvt Ltd, 11 Community Centre,
Panchsheel Park,New Delhi–110 017, India
Penguin Group (NZ), 67 Apollo Drive, Rosedale, Auckland 0632, New Zealand
(a division of Pearson New Zealand Ltd)
Penguin Books, Rosebank Office Park, 181 Jan Smuts Avenue,
Parktown North 2193, South Africa
Penguin China, B7 Jaiming Center, 27 East Third Ring Road North,
Chaoyang District, Beijing 100020, China

Penguin Books Ltd, Registered Offices: 80 Strand, London WC2R 0RL, England

First published in the United States of America by Viking Penguin,
a member of Penguin Group (USA) Inc. 2011
Published in Penguin Books 2012

3   5   7   9   10   8   6   4   2

THE LIBRARY OF CONGRESS HAS CATALOGED THE HARDCOVER EDITION AS FOLLOWS:
Johnson, Paul.
Socrates : a man for our times / Paul Johnson.
p. cm.
Includes bibliographical references and index.
ISBN 978-0-670-02303-5 (hc.)
ISBN 978-0-14-312221-0 (pbk.)
1. Socrates. I. Title.
B317.J65 2011
183'.2—dc23   2011019767

Printed in the United States of America
Set in Dante   Designed by Francesca Belanger

To S.B., guide, philosopher, and friend

CONTENTS

Socrates

I

Living Man and Ventriloquist's Doll

There is always a spirit of the times. Even in deep antiquity, strong and almost identical impulses drove forward the elites in societies separated by unbridged chasms of space. We cannot perhaps explain these coordinations. But we can profitably study them. Two and a half millennia ago, in the fifth century B.C., in three advanced areas, where literacy existed but was still in its infancy, three outstanding individuals echoed one another in insisting that the distinction between their civilizations and the surrounding barbarism must be reinforced by systematic moral education.

Confucius (a Latinized form of Kung Fu-tzu, meaning Philosopher Kung) was born in Shantung, China, in 551 B.C., dying aged seventy-three, in 479 B.C. He came from a poor but distinguished patrician family, whose descendants, in the seventy-sixth generation, still live in the district. He was a clever child and, while still a schoolboy, conceived the notion of devoting his life to the moral and cultural transformation of society by a new kind of educa-

5

tion. It was to stress all that was best in Chinese learning, based on six arts: ritual, calligraphy, arithmetic, and music, with the physical skills of archery and charioteering. His pupils recorded him saying: "At fifteen I set my heart on learning. At thirty I firmly took my stand as a teacher. At forty I had no delusions about education. At fifty I felt the Mandate of Heaven to teach. At sixty my ear was attuned to my pupils. At seventy I followed heart's desire without overstepping the boundaries of right."

It was Confucius's view, recorded by his pupils in what are called the Analects, that education was the key to everything: A person should be so deep in study that he forgets to eat, so full of joy in learning he ignores all practical worries, and so busy acquiring knowledge he does not notice old age coming on. Education was the process whereby civilization, and the minds and bodies of those privileged to enjoy it, breathed and lived.

In 458 B.C., the Hebrew priest and scribe Ezra returned to Jerusalem from Babylon. He had been born when Confucius was in his sixties and was the leading intellectual among the exiled Jewish community in Persia. He brought with him an edited and freshly transcribed version of the Pentateuch, the first five books of the Torah, or Jewish Bible, what Christians call the Old Testament. The word Torah came to mean "the Law," but its meaning originally, and certainly in Ezra's day, was instruction, teaching, guidance. Ezra used the Torah as the basis for the refoundation of the Jewish community in the Promised Land, after the dislocation of the Exile. It was his manual of instruction, as the rest of his life was one of those rare occasions in history when education was used as the means to reform an entire society, morally, politically, economically, and socially.

When Ezra began his mission, Socrates was twelve. He had been born in Athens, then a city-state democracy, in 470 B.C., nine years after Confucius's death. Whereas Ezra was of the priestly ruling elite, a direct descendant of Zadok, known in Hebrew history as the Priest, the archetypal hierarch, and Confucius was an aristocrat and magistrate, familiar with royal circles, Socrates was middle-class. His father was a mason and carver in stone, and his mother (he said) was a midwife. Socrates, thanks to his powerful intellect and still more to the way he employed it, contrived to make himself classless, the first classless person in history. Despite these different backgrounds, the three men were united by their passion for education, to which they devoted their lives. To all three, education involved learning all that was most valuable in their societies. But beyond knowledge, education was a process whereby virtue or the ability to lead a good life was acquired. And to cap it all, Socrates was in no doubt that education, by making one virtuous, was the surest road to happiness. He was the first seer we know of who pondered deeply on what makes humans happy and how such a blessing can be acquired.

Such a man is well worth knowing about, and for 2,500 years the learned and intellectually enterprising in all countries have sought to know him. At a superficial level, it is easy. Socrates is the quintessential philosopher, the seeker and conveyor of wisdom. But the more one penetrates from the superficial to the essence of the man, the more difficult it becomes. Socrates wrote nothing. Nor did Confucius. But whereas Confucius was listened to attentively by scholars who then collaborated to produce an exact transcript of his teaching—rather as in the twentieth century the pupils of Wittgenstein, another philosopher who wrote little, tried to remember and set down every word from his life—Socrates had a quite different experience. Two remarkable men attached themselves to him and sought to immortalize him in words. Xenophon was a country gentleman, a traveler-adventurer and a general who, thanks to Socrates, whom he venerated, became an amateur student of philosophy. He loved writing and, as countless generations of schoolchildren know, wrote a pure form of classical Greek admirably adapted for the classroom. He wrote the *Anabasis,* the best book on a single military experience to come down to us from antiquity, and among many other works, the most thorough manual on training horses in the classical library, as well as its companion volume on the use of cavalry. He also produced his *Memoirs,* a verbatim account of a dinner party in which Socrates is the central guest. All this is valuable, but it has to be said that Xenophon never comprehended and so could not reproduce the sheer power of Socrates' mind, its unique combination of steel, subtlety, and frivolity. If he were our sole authority for Socrates, we would never have learned to venerate him as the founder of philosophy as an expert science.

Our chief source, who sought with all his astounding ability as a writer and thinker to perpetuate the work of Socrates, was his pupil Plato. Plato was a genius, which is both our boundless delight and our misfortune. Being taught by Socrates was the central event of his life, and after his master's death he spent much of his remaining time recording what he said in a series of dialogues or conversations. More than a score have survived, plus two companion documents: Socrates' verbatim defense when on trial for his life, and a record of his last hours before his death sentence was carried out. These two documents, plus the earliest dialogues, are authentic records of Socrates the man, the historical seer at work.

However, Plato was not only a genius but one of a particular kind. He was a don, an academic. The very first academic, in fact, for after Socrates' death, he founded, in a suburban park in Athens, a study place—we would call it a think tank—called the Academy, from which the profession takes its name. It was the earliest university, and its prize alumnus, who came to Plato's classes when he was seventeen, was Aristotle, third of the sturdy tripod of masters on which the entire corpus of Western philosophy rests. Aristotle went on to found his own university, the Lyceum, in Athens as companion and rival to Plato's, so that the characteristic pattern of academic life, competitive animosity, was well established before the end of the fourth century B.C.

When writing his documents on Socrates' end, and his own early dialogues, Plato was still innocent enough, that is still sufficiently enraptured by Socrates' thinking and method, to reproduce both accurately. They form a trustworthy record of Socrates' enormous and vital contribution to the best way of using our mind to reach truth. But as Plato began to play his new role as academic, as the vesture of the don, the metaphorical cap and gown, settled comfortably on his head and shoulders, he underwent a transformation. To his persona as the first academic he added or superimposed the complementary persona of the first intellectual, by which I mean someone who thinks ideas matter more than people.

As an intellectual he began to formulate his own ideas. As an academic he quickly merged them into a system. And as a teacher he used Socrates to spread and perpetuate it. In his earlier writings Plato presented Socrates as a living, breathing, thinking person, a real man. But as Plato's ideas took shape, demanding propagation, poor Socrates, whose actual death Plato had so lamented, was killed a second time, so that he became a mere wooden man, a ventriloquist's doll, to voice not his own philosophy but Plato's. Being an intellectual, Plato thought that to spread his ideas was far more important than to preserve Socrates as a historic, integrated human being. Using Socrates as an articulate doll was, he saw, the easiest way to bring about this philosophical dispersal. So the act of transforming a living, historical thinker into a mindless, speaking doll— the murder and quasi-diabolical possession of a famous brain—became in Plato's eyes a positive virtue. That is the only charitable way of describing one of the most unscrupulous acts in intellectual history. Thus Plato, with no doubt the best intentions, created, like Frankenstein, an artificial monster-philosopher. It is particularly damaging to our understanding of Socrates in that the line of demarcation in Plato's writings between the real Socrates and the monster is unclear. It has been argued about for centuries, without any universally accepted result, and anyone who writes on the subject must make up their own mind, as I have done in this account.

Happily we have other sources, independent of Plato and Xenophon, which give us bits of information about Socrates. His contemporary, the comic dramatist Aristophanes, who also seems to have been a friend—but then, in showbiz is there such a thing as friendship?—wrote a savagely hostile play about him, *Clouds*. There is an account of Socrates by Diogenes Laertius, written seven hundred years later but using sources since lost to us. There are anecdotes, aperçus, recorded sayings, and snippets of information in the works of many classical and early medieval writers, from Cicero and Seneca, Plutarch and Lucian, to St. Augustine and Tertullian—and many others—who had access to libraries that were totally destroyed in the Dark Ages.

These bits and pieces help us to flesh out or correct the primary material Plato and Xenophon provide. But we always have to bear in mind the low regard classical and, still more, postclassical writers had for truth, their habitual inaccuracy even when trying to be honest, their lack of impartiality, historicity, or plausibility or even, one feels, common sense, and the slovenly way books were written, copied, and preserved. Before the coming of the codex or book proper, writing was done on papyrus rolls about thirty-three feet (ten meters) long. A roll might contain a book of Thucydides or two of Homer. But there was no uniformity, and scribes wrote for other scribes, not for the reader (they were strongly trade-unionized in every epoch and area). There was no attempt to stick to a specific number of letters to a line or lines to a column. Punctuation did not exist nor capital letters nor regular spacing between words, and a short stroke under a line, known as a *paragraphos*, was the only indication of a change of subject, pause, or, in plays and dialogues—very important for Plato's texts involving Socrates—a change of speaker, whose name, irritatingly, was hardly ever given. All these factors and many other slovenly habits increased the large number of textual errors inevitable in hand-copying, and as the manuscript chain stretched over centuries, even millennia, an incorrupt text became an impossibility. From the Renaissance onward, the prime task of generations of scholars until our own day has been to produce good texts. Even so, we have absolutely no guarantee that what we read of Socrates' sayings were

Plato's transcriptions of them, as set down 2,450 years ago. And all this is in addition to the loss of manuscripts in their entirety or in part. Until Socrates' time, no one who speculated about the cosmos and its inhabitants has been fortunate enough to have their conclusions survive. The works of pre-Socratic philosophers, as they are called, are quite literally fragments.

Nonetheless, Socrates himself is known to us as man and thinker, as a hugely real, living, and enjoyable human being. Let us meet him.

II

The Ugly Joker with the Gift for Happiness

Socrates was proud of being born an Athenian. He lived all his life in the city and never left it except in her service as a soldier. He was often critical of Athenian ways and leaders but never wavered in his conviction that it was the best of all city-states in which to live. And this, like most of his views, was sound and practical.

Greece in the fifth century B.C. was a collection of city-states, of which Athens was the largest and usually the richest and most powerful. Greece as a whole was innovative, enterprising, and above all, competitive, and Athens was the epicenter of the competitive spirit. Most cities held their own annual competitions, both athletic and cultural, but in addition there were Panhellenic games open to the entire Greek-speaking world: the Olympian, Pythian, Isthmian, and Nemean games. The most prestigious were the Olympian, held every four years at Olympia in the northwest Peloponnese.

We know a lot about these occasions. They were founded in 776 B.C., two centuries before Socrates' birth, and were held until A.D. 393, over a millennium later, when they were abolished as a pagan festival by the Christian Roman Emperor Theodosius I. And of course they were a pagan event for, like almost all Greek institutions, their origins were religious. Socrates was fond of reminding young men that the point of an Olympic victory was not the honor and money received by the victors, but service to god, in the shape of Zeus, whose magnificent giant statue of gold and ivory at Olympus was created during his lifetime by his friend Phidias. The race on foot the length of the stadium was the first and remained the chief event, but other tests of speed, strength, and endurance were added—including boxing, wrestling, a race for men in armor, and chariot and horse races. Both umpires and competitors took an oath of fair play and justice, but decisions were often challenged, and crowds booed and sometimes attacked the umpires. In early times, Sparta, the first city to train its athletes professionally, just as it took warfare with deadly seriousness, usually emerged the overall victor, but gradually other cities, not least Athens, produced fierce competition. Money began to talk. Socrates' rich young friend Alcibiades, for instance, entered six chariot teams for the Olympics, and carried off first, second, and fourth prizes. We know this because a complete list of the Olympic winners, from 776 B.C. to A.D.

217, was drawn up by Julius Africanus, and preserved by the church historian Eusebius.

The competitive spirit spread to every aspect of Greek life: poetry, drama, music, public speaking or rhetoric, and art. In most, Athens was incomparably the leader, and its annual city contests, especially in tragic and comic drama, were more important than any Panhellenic occasion. Socrates was concerned in such events, being a friend of Aristophanes, who won the first prize for comedy three times, and especially of Euripides, youngest of the three great Athenian tragedians. Euripides, though fifteen years Socrates' senior, came to him for advice, and there is a tradition that Socrates had a hand in his plays, perhaps with his trio containing *Hippolytus,* which won first prize in 428 B.C.

The competitive atmosphere in Athens and the pride Athenians took in their city were much enhanced by external events in the early years of Socrates' century. The Persian Empire, the greatest the world had ever known, west of China, was a constant threat to Greece, especially after Athens encouraged her fellow Ionian cities in what is now western Turkey to revolt against their Persian overlords. Persia invaded Greece but was repulsed by 10,000 Athenians at the Battle of Marathon (490 B.C.). According to Socrates' friend the historian Herodotus, the Persians lost 6,400 killed, against Athenian losses of 192, making it one of the great victories of antiquity. Among those who fought in the battle was Aeschylus, senior of the three great tragedians, and it is possible Socrates' father, Sophroniscus, was there too, as a hoplite or heavy infantryman.

The Persians invaded again in 480, in enormous strength—three hundred thousand men and six hundred ships. Despite heroic efforts by Leonidas and his three hundred Spartans, who died defending the pass of Thermopylae, the Persians pressed on, Athens was evacuated, and the city burned, the sacred buildings on the Acropolis being reduced to rubble. However, combined Spartan and Athenian forces routed the Persian army at the Battle of Plataea. Athens alone, under the leadership of Xanthippus, (father of Pericles, who was to dominate Athens for much of Socrates' life), won a decisive naval war, and by 479 Athens had established herself as the leading power among the Greeks. In 477 Athens founded the Delian League of Greek States, confirming her ascendancy and laying the basis for an Athenian Empire. By 463 B.C. Miltiades' son Cimon had ended any threat from Persia and the period of Athenian greatness had begun. By then Socrates was a boy of seven.

The city-state in which he grew up was by constitution and in spirit a democracy. The *polis,* or city, had long been identified with "the people in arms," the aristocracy providing the cavalry and the tradesmen, artificers, and other skilled workingmen forming the hoplites and owning their own armor and weapons. The basis of a democratic constitution had been laid down by Cleisthenes in the generation before Socrates was born, using the expression *isonomia*, or equality, to describe the rights of citizenship. More democratic measures were passed, when Socrates was a child, under the leadership of Ephialtes, though the fact that he was murdered in 462 B.C. indicates that politics, with its class-war overtone, was a serious, even brutal business, remaining so throughout Socrates' life.

The population of Athens varied greatly, depending on war, trade, and the economy. It is likely that when Socrates was born the total number of citizens, who had full rights to vote in the *ecclesia*, or assembly, to stand for office as general (*strategos*) or magistrate (*archon*), or to sit as jurymen, was a little over 120,000, rising to 180,000 in about 430 B.C., when he was entering middle age, and falling to perhaps 100,000 by his death. In addition, there were large numbers of *metics*, or resident aliens, some of whom held citizen rights, their ratio to born citizens ranging from one in six to two in five. Then there were slaves, who had no rights, varying from 30,000 to perhaps 100,000. But in all it is unlikely that the population of Athens, in Socrates' lifetime, ever exceeded 250,000. This was the population of Venice at its zenith and of London at the end of the seventeenth century; the entire population of the American colonies in 1700 was around 275,000.

Socrates therefore was born (in May) in what we would call a medium-size town. His *deme,* or district, was on the south side of the city. In the *Laches* dialogue of Plato we are told his father, Sophroniscus, was friends with the family of Aristides the Just, the Athenian statesman who was at various times chief magistrate, statesman, and army and naval commander, but was later exiled for two years and reduced to poverty. His father is also credited with various carvings on the Acropolis, but without firm evidence. His mother, Phaenarete, came from a "good" family and in the *Theaetetus* dialogue is said to have been a skillful midwife—not a professional one, of course, as such did not exist. Socrates was proud of her and did not at all mind jokes being made about her activities as an *accoucheuse,* as for instance in Aristophanes' *Clouds.* He was always interested in medicine and doctoring, bringing it into his dialogues, and it seems to me highly likely that he knew Hippocrates, the greatest doctor of ancient Greece, who was his exact contemporary and who evidently told Plato about medical science.

From the *Crito* dialogue we learn that his father gave

his son a good education at the gymnasium: reading, writing, athletics, music. Tradition says he went into his father's trade as a stone carver. The travel writer Pausanias (second century A.D.), the Baedeker of ancient Greece, says in his day a group of statues, *The Graces* on the Acropolis, was shown as Socrates' work, and this claim is repeated by Diogenes Laertius. But he may have been confused with another Socrates: it was a common name in fifth century B.C., and there were many stone carvers, for there was so much work for the trade in Athens, attracting masons from all over Greece and the Middle East. Socrates certainly held views on art. Sculptors, indeed, can be heavily sententious about it. Rodin could be a bore on the subject, as more recently could the Yorkshire-born Henry Moore. Socrates was never a bore—far from it—but Xenophon says he had a discussion on expressions in art with the sculptor Cleiton and the painter Parrhasius. "Nobility and dignity," he is recorded as saying, "self-abasement and servility, prudence and understanding, insolence and vulgarity, are all reflected in the face and in the attitudes of the body, whether still or in motion, and can be captured by the artist." This observation is all the more remarkable in that Socrates disliked allowing his emotions to show in his face. Four centuries later, Cicero, who seems to have known a lot about him, said that to show fears or appetites on your face was undignified: "Always keep the same expression, like Socrates."

While we do not know for sure if Socrates ever worked as a stone carver or whether he had any other manual occupation, we can be certain of one thing: He was a soldier, and an admirable one. This is attested by various references in Plato and Xenophon, and by other sources. Socrates had strong views about the use of force, as we shall see. But he was not a pacifist. Bertrand Russell's rejection of participation in World War I would have been alien to him, and he would have made short work of the specious arguments with which Russell sought to persuade others from serving (and which landed him in jail). As a citizen of Athens, which he loved, Socrates felt it a duty to fight her battles, in his middle rank as a hoplite. I think it likely he saw service as a young man, though there is no specific evidence of it. But we know he was at the siege of Potidaea, a strongly fortified port and former colony of Corinth. As a member of the Delian League, it was subject to Athenian leadership. Its tribute, or contribution to the common war fund, was increased to fifteen talents in 434 B.C. It revolted, and Athens besieged and reduced the city in 430 B.C., sending soldier-colonists (*cleruchs*) to occupy it. Socrates was there. He was then in his late thirties. He also fought at Amphipolis on the North Aegean coast, a place colonized by Athens in 437–436 B.C.—it was near the gold and silver mines of the Pangaean district and commercially important. In the early stages of the Peloponnesian War, Amphipolis surrendered to Sparta without a fight, and Athens went to a lot of trouble trying to get it back. The future historian Thucydides, then a young officer— he was ten years Socrates' junior—was involved at Amphipolis too. Both these great men, though they differed on many things, notably religion, agreed on their devotion to Athens and its importance, and Thucydides' clarity of historical causation and fair-mindedness may owe much to Socrates. But there is no clear evidence of their contact.

In 432 B.C. Socrates fought in the painful Athenian retreat from Potidaea. It was deep winter and bitterly cold. Socrates showed remarkable endurance and courage, all the more admirable because he was then forty-six, almost an old man by the normal reckoning of those days. We have eyewitness evidence of Socrates' conduct in this campaign from his young aristocratic friend Alcibiades. He makes three distinct points. First he says that Socrates saved his life by standing over him when he was wounded and driving off the enemy, regardless of his own safety. Second, he says that Socrates, fully armored and carrying his weapons, was a formidable figure, even in retreat. He says there was something about his bearing that made the enemy leave him severely alone: They sensed that if they had tried to seize him, they would have "met with desperate resistance." Third, he testified to Socrates' amazing hardiness. He wore thin clothing despite the cold and went barefoot even in the snow. No discomfort or shortage of food or drink seemed to dismay him. He was a splendid and cheerful campaigner.

Socrates' indifference to physical well-being—clothing, food, drink, warmth, and shelter, everything except company, which he always relished and needed—was a characteristic throughout his life and is well attested by a variety of sources. It seems to have been partly temperament and partly self-training. He decided early in life to be a teacher or, as he would have put it, an "examiner" of men and that such was to be his occupation but not his profession: He would take no pay. Hence one of his objects was to reduce his needs to an absolute minimum. He took delight in this process, deliberately nourishing negative appetites. He observed the shop displays in the Athens agora (marketplace) and said, "How many things I can do without!" He also liked to observe the prices, and exclaim: "How expensive Athens is!" then, the next moment, "How cheap Athens is!" Various sayings survive in different forms: "Some men live to eat. I eat to live." "Hunger is the best *aperitif*." "I only drink when I am thirsty." When someone offered him land to build a house, "Would you give me leather to make shoes?" "Greedy people don't appreciate delicacies." He kept fit in the stadium and gymnasia: "A healthy body is the greatest of blessings." He "frequently danced," saying, "It is good for me." He did not disdain drinking, in company, but was never seen drunk. But there is an image of him, at a feast, drinking from a large, wide vessel known as the Silver Sea. He said, "Those who drink a lot don't relish rare wines." Asked "What makes a young man virtuous?" he replied, "Avoiding excess in anything." He said, "Poverty is a shortcut to self-control." And "Leisure is the most valuable of possessions." And "Nothing is to be said in favor of riches and high birth, which are easy roads to evil."

Socrates was, by the standards of Greece in the fifth century B.C., an ugly man. For the Greeks set a high value on regularity of features and a head and face we would call Byronic. Alcibiades, a spectacularly handsome man, compared Socrates to Silenus. Socrates said the same. He did not mind the comparison at all. Silenus represented, among men, the spirit of the wilderness, being half animal. The satyrs were similar. These creatures were the organic origin of Athenian comedy, and the first comics wore Silenus masks on the stage. These and the stone portraits of Silenus that have survived (usually in Roman copies) are remarkably similar to stone, marble, or bronze representations of Socrates that have come down to us, in copies of copies. It is likely that, soon after Socrates' death, a bronze statue was made of him for Athens to set up in a public place in expiation of the crime the city had committed against him. Many Roman copies, usually in marble, survive. Often the body is missing and only the head survives. There is one in Berlin, another in Copenhagen. In the Borghese Gallery, Rome, there is a composite statue, of which the arms and hands and other bits are modern, the head Roman. All these are Silenus-type in face but with human ears. Two are inscribed SOCRATES. There is also, in the British Museum, an alabaster statuette of Socrates, probably from Alexandria, a Roman copy of a Greek fourth-century-B.C. bronze.

These all confirm the information from literary sources that Socrates was bearded, hairy, with a flat, spreading nose, prominent, popping eyes, and thick lips. In Xenophon's *Symposium,* he is recorded as challenging Critobulus to a contest in beauty. As usual, he was joking, speaking with his customary tone of irony and self-deprecation. The dialogue begins, "Why, Critobulus, do you flaunt your looks, as if you were more handsome than me?" "Oh, I know I am inferior to you in beauty, Socrates, and therefore I must be even uglier than Silenus." Socrates continues, using his usual method of cross-questioning: "Are only men handsome?" "No. A horse or a bull can be handsome. Even a shield." "How is it that such different things can all be handsome?' "Because they are well made, by art or nature, for their purpose." "What are eyes for?" "To see." "For that reason my eyes are more handsome than yours." "How so?" "Yours can see only in a direct line. Mine can do that but sideways too, because they stick out so." "And is your nose better shaped than mine?" "Yes, if God made the nose for smelling, for your nostrils are turned down, whereas mine are wide and turned up and can receive smells from every direction." "I grant you your mouth is better, for if God gave us mouths to eat yours is big enough to gobble three times as much as mine." "Yes, and my kisses are more sweet and luscious than yours since my lips are so big and thick."

Socrates, then, was ugly, and later in life he developed a paunch. He had a tendency to be bow-legged and walked in a sideways motion. As he was in the streets every day, he became an unmistakable figure in Athens, and for many a comic one, even disreputable. Sometimes he was mocked and even jostled. Asked why he did not resent such treatment, he replied, "If a donkey kicks you, do you take legal action against him?" Or: "If a man slaps my face, he does me no evil, only himself." As Alcibiades noticed during the retreat from Delium, Socrates was imperturbable. He exuded serenity. There were many things he deplored, but nothing left him depressed. If he was angry, he never showed it—except, in contrast to most people, who raise their voices in anger, he lowered his, and spoke quietly. He was genial, and reminds me of Lord Holland, of whom the poet Thomas Moore said, "He came down to breakfast every morning looking as though he had just received a tremendous stroke of good fortune." To those who knew Socrates, he was impossible to dislike and difficult not to love.

There may have been one exception: his wife. Or, possibly, wives. It is notorious that exceptionally good public figures are difficult to live with. When Lady Longford, married to the famous philanthropist and do-gooder Frank Longford, was questioned on this point, she said, "What do we call the wife of a saint?" and answered herself: "A martyr." There are confusing tales that Socrates had an earlier (or later, or bigamous) marriage to a woman called Myrto. If she gave birth to children, they are unrecorded even in traditional stories. What we do know is that he had, at the time of his death, a wife called Xanthippe and had three children by her. He had evidently married her late in life, possibly already over fifty. At the time of his death, aged seventy, the eldest was only a youth of about seventeen or eighteen, and the others younger still. One may have been a child in arms. When Xanthippe, as we know, spent Socrates' last night with him in the jail, she had a child with her, presumably because he was too young to be left alone. Plato and Xenophon, our two best sources, say nothing against Xanthippe's character. But various traditions present her as a shrew, who shouted at Socrates and gave him a hard time. Why had he married her instead of a more docile woman? He answered, "Because we know from the business of horse training that owners often like to pick a difficult animal, which poses more interesting problems." Could he live happily with her? "Yes, and it proves I could live happily with anyone." She was a splendid subject for his jokes, as when, having bawled him out at length, inside the house, she poured a basin of slops on him from the roof. He said, "As always, the thunder is followed by rain." So far as I can see, he was perfectly content with her, and it is notable (for the age) that he was still having sex with her and begetting children in his late sixties. Xanthippe must have contributed to his high opinion of the ability of women and to his belief that in most matters they were the equal of men. My belief is that their life together was happy.

What strikes one most about Socrates as a human being, however, is not just his opinions, often unusual, even revolutionary, and his personality, which was riveting to those who came close to it, but his reciprocal delight in the people and city of Athens. If ever a man was at home in the place where he was born, lived, and died, it was Socrates the Athenian. All the more so in that Athens was going through the most glorious, exciting, and dangerous phase in its history. Let us look more closely at this remarkable city.

III

Socrates and the Climax
of Athenian Optimism

Socrates often reminds one of Sir Thomas More, combining as he did absolute rectitude with puckish humor and a patriotism qualified only by his profound sense of religious duty. More said, "I serve the king—but God first." Socrates said, "Athenians, I cherish and love you. But I shall obey God rather than you." It was Socrates' good fortune that he came to maturity when Athens, which had successfully brought the whole of Greece to overwhelming victory against the mighty Persian Empire, was reaching its splendid but lonely apogee. There are such rare moments in history. In 1940 Churchill told the British—I heard him say it—"Let us therefore brace ourselves to our duty, and so bear ourselves that, if the British Commonwealth and its empire last for a thousand years, men will still say, 'This was their finest hour.'"

Greece, in the mid-fifth century B.C., like Britain in 1940, had a leader who embodied everything it seemed to stand for, and who articulated its message to all the world and to posterity. Pericles (495–429 B.C.) was arguably the greatest statesman of antiquity. He was son of Xanthippus, who had plunged up and down the roller-coaster of Athenian politics at the time, round the turn of the sixth and fifth centuries B.C., when Cleisthenes had founded Athenian democracy. Agariste, Pericles' mother, was the great man's niece, and he aspired to complete his great-uncle's work by perfecting the city's democratic system. The victory over Persia filled Athens, and Pericles in particular, with a spirit of optimism that he put to practical use by devising immense schemes of progress. He was rich, and we first hear of him as a theatrical angel, or choregus, financing Aeschylus' stupendous tragedy *Persae*, commenting on the Athenian victory, produced in 472 B.C., two years before Socrates' birth. Ten years later, he was elected chief magistrate and continued to be so for a generation. It was Pericles' gift to transmute Athenian optimism into a spirit of constructive energy and practical dynamism that swept through this city like a controlled whirlwind. Pericles believed that Athenians were capable of turning their brains and hands to anything of which human ingenuity was capable—running a city and an empire, soldiering, naval warfare, founding a colony, drama, sculpture, painting, music, law, philosophy, poetry, oratory, education, science—and do it better than anyone else. Do it, moreover, in a mood of joyful freedom.

It was Pericles' good fortune not only to come to power at exactly the right time, but to be attended by a passionate admirer who was also a writer and historian of genius. Thucydides was born in 460 B.C., making him ten years younger than Socrates but to all intents his contemporary, who died in the same year. He was the perfect historian: He saw events more accurately and objectively, inquired more pertinaciously, and recorded them more truthfully than any other historian of antiquity. But he also felt himself involved, had strong opinions, and worshipped Pericles—as Plato worshipped Socrates a generation later—because he, too, loved energy and the dynamism it makes possible. Whereas Churchill wrote his own history, Pericles—who might have done so—was cut short by the plague. But he had Thucydides to do it for him. Perhaps its highest point was the funeral oration Pericles was appointed by Athens to pronounce over his dead soldiers after the first year of the Peloponnesian War. This was a grand and solemn occasion, attended by the elite and the populace of the city. Socrates was certainly there, alongside the dramatic poets Sophocles and Euripides, the architect-sculptor Phidias, and the painter Zeuxis.

It was the underlying theme of Pericles' panegyric over the dead that human beings were not the helpless victims of fate but masters of their own destiny. The soldiers had died defending Athens, which was the supreme human artifact. Then, being more explicit, he said Athens was the one society where justice applied equally to all, where men might not be equal but where social differences did not stop anyone getting to the top if he had enough ability. All Athenians voluntarily submitted to law and government, which they ultimately controlled, and this included fighting to defend it and, if necessary, dying, as these soldiers had done.

Athens was thus a disciplined, indeed a self-disciplined society, but its discipline was balanced by intellectual freedom. Society was open, the exercise of power transparent—there was no secrecy by authority and so no suspicion among those who freely submitted to it. Hence Athenian society was a model to other Greeks—"the School of Hellas"—and if it controlled other cities, it did so on its merits, and its subjects had no reason to complain of its rule any more than the soldiers who died to preserve it. This remarkable speech was faithfully recorded by Thucydides (who no doubt embellished and polished it), and it gave Socrates much food for thought as it raised so many issues on which he had strong opinions of his own, as we shall see. Not least, it illustrated the distinction he drew between oratory, which sought to persuade, and philosophy, which sought truth. That Pericles was persuasive was abundantly evident. But was what he said true?

The question was all the more important in that Pericles, in proclaiming his grandiose visions of Athenian humanism, was not alone. He was leader of a pleiad, a cluster of stars, gifted men of all kinds united by their high opinion of human capacity. They included the elderly Aeschylus, who died in 456 B.C., five years after Pericles swept to power, but whose *Prometheus Bound*, his last, unfinished play, tells the story of the mythical figure punished by Zeus for giving mankind fire and the arts. Prometheus is presented as the champion of the oppressed and a highly independent thinker, and this grand play, enormously exciting for Socrates—whose sympathies were strongly for and against its protagonist—was often revived in his lifetime. Also in the humanist circle was Sophocles (496–406 B.C.) who, though a quarter century older than Socrates, was known to him all his life and whose *Antigone* (441 B.C.), a desperate tragedy of cruelty, suicide, and despair, shows humans at their noblest and is a hymn to man and woman. It was so successful that Pericles put the playwright on his ticket when he next stood as *strategos*, and Sophocles was elected general in 440 B.C., the first of many public services he rendered in the intervals between his writing.

The most important of the pleiad, both in Pericles' eyes and in the view of Athens generally, was Protagoras (485–415 B.C.), who came from Abdera in Thrace but who made Periclean Athens his headquarters and taught there as a sophist from 455 B.C. He was the chief theorist and articulator of the Periclean doctrine of anthropocentrism and is quoted by Plato in his *Theaetetus* as laying down the maxim "Man is the measure of all things." His books, *On Truth* and *On the Gods*, have not survived, but the second came as close to atheism as was possible in ancient Greece. He was quoted as saying, "As for the gods I have no means of knowing whether they exist or not. Or what they are like in form. Many things prevent us knowing about them, including the sheer difficulty of the subject, and the brevity of human life." Socrates, like most Athenians, was not happy about that or about the fact that Protagoras taught *arete,* or virtue, to young men of rich or noble families, and taught it in a worldly way, as the means to "get on." He also charged high fees and became rich. Inevitably Protagoras and Socrates came to verbal blows in the fertile and fascinating dialogue named after Protagoras. This reveals him as urbane and reasonable and Socrates as unworldly and reasonable, the two philosophers competing to proclaim "progressive" views, Protagoras being particularly innovatory. He sets forth the view that criminal

justice should not be guided by revenge or retribution:
The aim of any punishment ought to be to deter the criminal and others from committing further crimes. This was
a theme Socrates was to develop with huge historical consequences, as we shall see. This dialogue is one of the best
Plato records. I do not want to anticipate Socrates' methods of arguing and teaching, which I will come to later.
But Protagoras posed him an unusual problem, for unlike
most of the clever men Socrates met and debated with,
Protagoras was highly rational, moderate and what Jane
Austen would have called "a sensible man." His worldli-
ness, though distasteful to Socrates, bringing forth his
most biting irony, was displayed with a disarming veneer
of common sense as well as considerable acumen. That
was exactly the combination Pericles valued. He ordered
him to give public lectures on progress and, in 443 B.C., to
draw up a working constitution for the new Athenian
colony of Thurii.

It was Pericles' view, reflecting a deep-rooted Athenian
conviction, that the civilized life of a polis was a whole,
and that the sensible citizen should, as a matter of duty to
his city and to himself, participate in every aspect of it.
Greek cities were planned, perhaps the first in history to
be arranged in an intelligent and purposeful fashion. By
the fifth century B.C., the Greeks had adopted the grid

structure developed in parts of the Middle East, and this made planning easier. The defensive core of the city, like the Acropolis of Athens, might be dictated by geography and geology. But within certain limits, the city could be made rational. All the facilities—assembly room, theater, lyceum (for music), the various gymnasia or schools, the stadium, and the agora or shopping center—were placed in convenient relationship to one another. And all were usually capable of accommodating the entire adult male citizenship.

Athens was a mobile society, upward and sideways. A young slave called Pasion, born when Socrates was forty, worked hard and intelligently at the bank where he ran errands, won his freedom, later parlayed his way into getting citizenship from the Assembly, or possibly bought it, and ended up the richest man in Greece, becoming unpopular enough to merit angry speeches from Demosthenes and Isocrates (his famous Trapeziticus or "Speech Against the Banker"). Again, in Socrates' time, a champion wrestler became a well-known philosopher. Playwrights and historians became generals; and generals, historians. Poets became statesmen, and politicians wrote plays. An architect might found a colony, and a man who made lamps might rule the city. Plato nearly devoted his life to poetry. Socrates thought seriously about going into public life before rejecting the idea at a sign from heaven "which coincided with my reason." Athens in the fifth century B.C. was unique in history in making it so easy for men of talent to cross professional and vocational boundaries.

It was also unique, at least in Pericles' heyday, in blending democracy, empire, and cultural triumph, indeed triumphalism. The secret was money. The Delian League, originally formed to fight Persia, became the basis for an Athenian empire of allies and colonies, each of which contributed to a common treasury held in Athens. Some rebuilding had taken place in the city to make good the damage inflicted by the Persian sacking. But Pericles, once installed in power, formed a scheme to use the common funds to rebuild Athens, especially its Acropolis, in the most splendid manner. The centerpiece was the erection of the Parthenon at the highest point of the Acropolis to house a gigantic gold and ivory statue of the goddess Athena. He claimed that the money was being spent in the interest of all the city-states forming the alliance, since Athena was the protectress of each one, and all looked to Athens and its glories, as Greeks still do, as epitomizing the Greek spirit of civilization. But others felt the money was being misapplied, especially whenever Athens felt the need to raise the tribute levied on each city. It is a common problem of supposedly liberal empires, whether taxes are raised to benefit all, as the mother country claims, or in fact benefit her alone. It formed a thread of argument that ran through the history of the British Empire and was the source of Britain's dispute with the thirteen American colonies, leading to the Revolutionary War and the founding of the United States.

At all events, Pericles pressed ahead and spent the money, in the process making Athens the artistic and architectural center of the ancient world, attracting craftsmen, and particularly skilled stone carvers, from all over Greece, and beyond. This was of particular interest for Socrates, for it was the family trade, and tradition has it that both he and his father shared in the work. More likely, in my view, he was fascinated by the Parthenon project because of the technical and, indeed, philosophic problems it raised. Pericles put in overall charge of the cultural and building program his friend and supporter Phidias (490–432 B.C.), who occupied the same role in the regime as Michelangelo did to Pope Julius II, Charles Le Brun to Louis XIV, or Baron Haussmann to Napoléon III. This brilliant man could turn his hand to painting or building or anything else requiring artistic skill, judgment, and grand ideas, but his chief work was as a sculptor. He had already created a bronze statue of Athena ten meters high, placed on a prominent part of the Acropolis. She was known as the Champion, and when the morning sun caught her helmet and spear tip, she could be seen by sailors as they rounded Cape Sunium twenty miles away, letting them know they were almost home.

Phidias now set about making a gigantic gold and ivory (or chryselephantine, as it was known) representation of Athena, as the climax of the restored Acropolis, together with a suitably grand and decorative temple to house it, the Parthenon. The statue's face, arms, and other visible flesh were composed of ivory, but many parts were made of solid gold, some of them concealed. The function of the work was not only to astonish the world but to house in holy safety Athens's gold reserve, for the hidden parts could be raided in time of need. Phidias's Athena, therefore, was the Central Bank of the city-state, as well as its presiding deity.

The Parthenon, which housed this precious cult figure, was the culminating masterpiece of the Doric order, a style of stone building that the Greeks had copied from pharaonic Egypt (though they would not admit it) and hugely improved. It was monumentally simple and, by the fifth century B.C., archaic and therefore suitable for a solemn religious building on the largest possible scale.

This enormous work was begun in 447 B.C. and dedicated, complete, a decade later, in 438 B.C. The working architect of the Parthenon was Ictinus, assisted by a man called Callicrates and another called Carpion. We know nothing of these two, but Ictinus was an able fellow, creator of the splendid Temple of Apollo at Bassae in Arcadia and also a writer, for he provided (according to a treatise on architecture written by the Roman engineer Vitruvius) an account of the building.

It is a pity this work has not survived, for the Parthenon raised, in magnificent form, two philosophical problems, which is why it was so important to Socrates. The first was the way in which architects created an illusory tension and excitement in their buildings by almost imperceptible deviations from the straight line. This art or science is called entasis and comes from the Greek verb *enteinein,* which conveys the idea of opposing forces holding an object in their power. Greek architects of the fifth century B.C. would have agreed with Albert Einstein's dictum on space-time: "Everything is slightly curved." By minute deviations from straight lines working in conjunction with arcs of wide radials in all three planes, by a slight upward curvature of the stylobate, echoed in the entablature, by thickened corner columns and double contractions of corner intercolumniations, and by many other such devices the Parthenon was made to seem more "real" and was given a sense of movement, of organic life. The measurements involved to produce these effects had to be exact and added an extra dimension to the work of architects, draftsmen, carvers, and stonemasons. When Socrates insisted that mathematics should be used for practical purposes (not the metaphysical speculations that his pupil Plato came to propound), the building of the Parthenon, which he had observed from start to finish, was exactly what he had in mind.

Socrates was also fascinated, as various dialogues recorded by both Plato and Xenophon indicate, by the whole process of illusion in art, and entasis is one of its subtlest applications. We have to assume that Phidias, in consultation with Pericles, was responsible for what architects now call these "refinements," for they added considerably to the cost. At the Parthenon, the upward curvature in the east *krepidoma* and the batter or inverted inclination of the exterior planes of walls were amazing and expensive features. Indeed this great building marked the climax of optical sophistication in the architecture of antiquity. The deflections, while adding enormously to the difficulty of erecting the Parthenon, which was made throughout from the finest marble, greatly enhanced its beauty and stability, and explains why, despite the efforts of barbarians, Turks, Venetian artillerymen, and others, it has somehow survived two and a half millennia.

Paul Johnson

The Parthenon was embellished, inside and out, by sculpture of the highest quality, under Phidias's watchful eye, and occasional master hand and chisel. The best of it was saved by Lord Elgin and can still be seen, gloriously displayed, in the British Museum. In its entirety it marks the culmination of the art of ancient Greece, and no more need be said here—except on one point, of great interest to Socrates. Greek temples were the homes of the gods, and their decorations, outside and within, portrayed the activities of immortals. That was a religious duty and an inflexible artistic convention. However, in the Parthenon, the frieze shows a procession of mortals: Athenian citizens moving in their ranks to honor Athena. This is the first and one of the few surviving examples where a gathering of mortal men and women, albeit for a sacred purpose, is represented on a Greek temple. All others portray gods or heroic mythology. That this innovation was deliberate and authorized at the highest level we cannot doubt, and it marked the most adventurous point of Periclean humanism. To Socrates it must have been the most significant feature of the entire cultural enterprise that Pericles launched.

We look at these marble figures, in the British Museum and elsewhere, and admire the majestic monumentality of the Parthenon in respectful silence. But such images need to be seen in their aural context of poetry and music. We should never try to conjure up the spirit of Socrates in silence. The Greeks had ascended from barbarism by creating civilized, controlled, and disciplined sounds, whether spoken in poetry, sung in chorus, or sung solo to the accompaniment of various instruments, especially the stringed lyre and the flute, or twin-piped aulos. Greeks recited or sang poetry long before they learned to write prose, and music was a form of moral training centuries before their thinkers turned to ethics.

In the fifth century B.C. the Greeks, conscious of the enormous emotional power of music, began to investigate systematically its intellectual aspects. Pythagoras, in what is now Italy, discovered the relationship between musical intervals and mathematics, and in Athens, Damon became almost the first to write extensively on music, especially about the ethical effects on people of various rhythms and scales. Both Damon and his teacher Prodicus were well known to Socrates and esteemed by him; and Plato, whom Socrates introduced to the whole subject of musical ethics, had much to say on the subject when he came to write, especially the *Republic*.

Socrates, I suspect, had a poor musical ear. Although he knew that a man seeking wisdom and virtue ought to attend to music, he found it hard to do so. He exculpated himself by arguing that philosophy was the finest kind of music. In old age he aspired to learn the lyre, the instrument most accessible to amateurs, as the guitar is for us today. He never doubted the importance of music and listened to Damon earnestly. It is significant that Damon had been Pericles' tutor. Music offered a unique means to involve large numbers of citizens of both sexes and all ages in public events. There were endless religious processions, with singing and musical accompaniment. A special building, the Pompeion, near the Dipylon Gate of Athens, was erected at the spot where processions assembled. Virgins carried sacred implements at the head of the procession. Old men bore green branches. Youths led sacrificial animals. Often chariots and men on horseback followed. Marshals kept order. An orchestra was part of all processions.

Pictures on pottery—our chief window on fifth-century Athens—give us illuminating glimpses of ceremonial music. A black-figure Attic amphora done thirty years before Socrates was born, now in the Munich Gallery of Antique Art, shows such a band of aulos and kithara (the professional form of lyre), barbitos (a bass lyre), and clappers—the clapper man dancing. Instrumentalists were usually men—women specialized in the harp, which was too large to be portable—but men, women, boys, and girls sang in the choirs. The lyre had originally been made from the shell of a tortoise, which formed the soundbox, but this had been replaced by wood in Socrates' day. The kithara was more substantial, its arms prolonging the soundbox, and being big and heavy had to be held against the body, with a strap running over the shoulders and a band attached to the left wrist to steady it. A lyre, being much lighter, could be played by women. We also see them on pottery playing the aulos.

Only about a thousand bars of ancient Greek music has survived (some of them carved on rock), but Aristoxenus, a musical theorist born a generation after Socrates' death, says the notes covered three octaves and were grouped in five vocal headings, corresponding to bass, baritone, tenor, alto, and soprano, the last two often sung by children. Music was of several different types: processionals, with a strong beat of various speeds; religious hymns; comic hymns to Dionysus called dithyrambs, sung under the influence of alcohol and male-only; and paeans, songs of praise to gods and goddesses and to heroes, both mythical and contemporary.

The paean flourished under Pericles, who liked to add a triumphant, even military note to public occasions. He usually had himself sculpted wearing a helmet, visor lifted, showing his stern, handsome features: There is a fine Roman copy of a fifth-century-B.C. bronze original in the British Museum. But thanks to his efforts, music became a much more important element in Athenian life, and in Socrates' time we begin to hear of professional composers: Cinesias, Timotheus, Philoxenus, Melanippides, though not one of their notes survives. Greece had held musical competitions for some time, at Delphi, for instance, for the Pythian Games: One of Pindar's odes celebrates the victory of an aulos player. But Pericles created the Panathenaea music festival at Athens, which included prizes for every kind of music, including solo singing to the kithara and aulos, and the solo playing of both. Socrates' eventual interest in music and its ethical implications reflects this increase in quality and variety.

The dynamism of Pericles' cultural revolution likewise affected the theater, though it is misleading to draw any clear distinction between music and drama, even though the Athenian theater and the Odeon were two separate buildings, for most musical performances had dramatic elements, and nothing performed on the stage was without a musical element, before and after and often during the dramatic recitations. The Greeks did not feel there was much difference between the rhythm of their music and their poetical meters. The original essence of the drama was the chorus, chanted or sung. The unit was not the metrical foot but the phrase, and poets built up phrases of their choral lyrics into complex stanzas. The Greeks had always produced poets, long before they became literate. And all poetry was religious in origin: That is, it dealt with the actions of gods and their relations with men and women. Poets recited their works, which they knew by heart of course—a tradition still valid in England, for example, in the days of Coleridge and Wordsworth. And the audience learned them by heart too, in part; sometimes whole, even in Socrates' day. He refers to a friend who could recite the whole of the *Iliad*. Homer's works were quasi-religious, the nearest equivalent the Greeks had to the Jewish Torah, since they not only recounted their history but taught, after a fashion, manners and morals, too.

The theater was also religious in origin, springing from the cult of Dionysus. This half-human, half-animal, tragicomic, bibulous, and satyr-like god, springing from a barbarous tribal past, has no equivalent in Judeo-Christian religion and is difficult for us to understand. Yet his hold on the Greek cultural imagination was very powerful, and the fact that Socrates had a strong facial and bodily resemblance to caricatures of the god was an important source of his fascination to Athenians, his popularity and his unpopularity. They could not take their eyes off him when he held forth. Dionysus stood for the aspect of religion we would call fundamentalist or evangelical: highly emotional, noisy, singing, clapping, shouting, and dancing. Its solemnity was heavily qualified by wine-drinking, especially by the men. The women went into ecstatic convulsions and were then known as maenads. They wore human masks. This was the true origin of the drama, which in time bifurcated into comic and tragic performances.

Initially music played a dominant role, and the main performers were the chorus. In both its moods, it was much closer to what we would call an oratorio than a play. In the original Dionysiac drama, the dithyramb to the god was a hymn in the form of an ode, and the action was a service of worship, the chorus being the Athenian people doing homage to their god. Gradually the Dionysiac element diminished, then disappeared, clinging on only in the comedies as a species of masked buffoonery. Meanwhile plays appeared in which both the action and the lyrics presented in dramatic form stories from Greek myths and legends that were essentially tragic, the chorus providing narrative commentary and pointing morals. There were religious dramas throughout Socrates' lifetime and well into the fourth century B.C., for the subject matter was the relations between humans and the gods who controlled their destiny.

Some Greeks were coming to believe in the idea of eternal life and the immortality of the soul—it was a cen-

tral theme of Socrates' thinking—and the Dionysian theater, certainly in its tragic form, gave a spur to these
beliefs, as Dionysus was the Lord of Souls. Similar notions
of eternity and soul salvation were stirring in other civilized societies in the fifth century B.C., especially in Egypt
and still more in Hebrew Palestine. The Hebrews even
developed a form of drama as a result of these forces, a
notable example being the Book of Job, which has survived because it found its way into the canonical writings.
Scholars seem to think its date was around 400 B.C., the
time of Socrates' death, when Greek tragic drama had ma-
tured but was still religious. With its mocking chorus,
Job's dialogue with God, and its tremendous descriptions
of the natural world, Job is essentially a play about the
mysterious workings of God's providence, and it is poetry
intended to be recited in public—all characteristic of
Greek fifth-century-B.C. drama. It would be surprising if it
was not influenced by the Greek religious theater, as were
no doubt other Hebrew plays now lost to us. There is no
evidence I know of that Jews visited Athens or lived there
in Socrates' time, but plenty of Greeks lived in Palestine.

We now see this tragic poetry of Athens, usually en-
acted first in the Theater of Dionysus, as Greece's greatest
contribution to world literature, Homer alone excepted. It
was changing and maturing throughout the fifth century

B.C. but Pericles' cultural program hugely accelerated its development. Competition became annual, and substantial prizes were awarded. There were in consequence a large number of playwrights, but the stage was dominated by three. The earliest and historically the founder of the genre was Pericles' favorite, Aeschylus (525–456 B.C.), who had fought at the Battle of Marathon and probably Salamis, too. He was a passionate Athenian religious patriot. He won many competitions in his lifetime, and his plays continued to receive prizes after his death, but only 7 out of 70 to 80 have survived. We have only 7 by Sophocles (496–406) too, though he wrote 136, and 96 secured first or second prizes (he was never third). Euripides (485–406) was more fortunate: We have the texts of 19 of his plays out of 92, and he, too, won prizes.

According to Aristotle, who wrote at length about the theater, it was invented by Thespis, a sixth-century writer who introduced a solo actor who alternated with the chorus. Aeschylus built on this innovation and had two actors, three in his late plays, though it was Sophocles who brought in the third actor. Soon there were four or more, and as the actors multiplied, the role of the chorus, originally dominant, declined. It became a mere episode between scenes, like our curtain, and by the end of the fifth century B.C. had ceased to have anything to do with the play, being a mere musical punctuation mark. The religious element declined, too, after the death of Aeschylus, and the mythical heroes and heroines were developed into real-life characters. Sophocles and, still more, Euripides invented episodes, and toward the end of the century a new playwright, Agathon, who won his first victory in 416 B.C., when still a young man, invented entire plays, such as his *Antheus*, though only forty of his lines have survived. Plato's *Symposium* about Socrates was to celebrate this victory.

In Socrates' day there was no such thing as a purpose-built theater, like the magnificent one at Epidaurus, with its superb acoustics, which allow someone in the back row to hear whispers on the stage. Everything took place in broad daylight, though some scenes were set at night. Sophocles introduced stage scenery, and soon actors entered and left through doors, though there was no upper stage until the fourth century, after Socrates' death. Plays were taken with increasing seriousness and great efforts were made to judge the competitions fairly. Athens was divided into ten districts (originally tribes), and names of winners from each were sealed in an urn. But Plato says that decisions of judges were usually determined by the amount of applause from the audience.

It is clear that Socrates, Plato, and later Aristotle were

deeply concerned in theatrical developments, and there was a special reason for this. Greek tragedy in the fifth century showed a growing interest in human nature, in character and behavior under stress. While Aeschylus tends to present types—though there are notable individuals too—Sophocles specialized in noble individuals under appalling pressures, and Euripides often investigates unusual or extreme mentalities. What Athenians were beginning to see on the stage were not just bodies but embodied souls. This was very much Socrates' world, for he was a psychologist as well as a philosopher. But in general, tragic playwrights and philosophers were moving in the same territory, and it is not surprising that Plato, when still much influenced by Socrates, almost became a tragic poet. He would have made a good one. We know that Socrates as an old man wrote poetry, though none has survived. But we are told that a play by Euripides was "patched up" by him. A man who could successfully doctor a work by a leading playwright obviously was a constant playgoer and thoroughly familiar with the medium.

Socrates, thanks to his Dionysiac appearance, sense of irony, wit, and critical approach to almost every aspect of life, was obviously a man capable of patching up a comedy, too, though there is no evidence he ever did so. Primitives, not only in Greece, like pretending to be somebody else in public, and doing grotesque, obscene, and comic things they would not dare to do in normal life. We know from inscriptions that a humorous adult male chorus was an archaic element in Athens's Dionysiac feasting. An Attic black figure amphora from the sixth century B.C. shows men disguised as horses, mounted by other men, masked, with an accompanying flute player. Another, later one shows them dressed as birds. Vases from this time show dancing men wearing phalluses, and a krater from Corinth displays masked dancers with giant bellies strapped on. Enormous phalluses were carried in Dionysiac processions, and Aristotle writes of bawdy, comic verses, crude sex jokes, and what he calls "phallic songs"—he says they were still "customary to many cities," but no longer in Athens, which had become too sophisticated. Another feature was the crude abuse of audiences. This is a ploy used in our own day by American comics, and it was the great stock-in-trade of Aristide Briand, the Montmartre nightclub singer, lovingly drawn by Toulouse-Lautrec. The Old Comedy of the fifth century B.C., as historians call it, would have struck us as more like charades or a variety show than a play. There were lots of talking animals as in children's stories and folklore.

Aristophanes (445–385 B.C.), about whom we know little, though he figures in the famous Socratic dinner party recorded by Plato, transformed this theatrical ragbag of tricks into satiric plays, of which eleven survive (plus the titles and fragments of thirty-two more). Part of a play of his called *The Banqueters*, written when he was eighteen, survives, and it won a second prize. In the next two years, 426 and 425, he won first prize with the *Babylonians* (lost) and *Acharnians*, the first play of his to survive. This is about war and peace and is intended to be serious, though there are comic elements. Aristophanes, though classed as a comic playwright, in fact always hovers precariously between huge exaggerations of actual events and real people, and buffoonery. He is really a satirist, in the proper sense of the term. *Knights* (424 B.C.), the first play he produced himself (hitherto he had been classed as too young under the rules) and which, probably for this reason, won the first prize, was an attack on the reigning demagogue, Cleon. *Wasps* (422) is a satire on the Athenian jury system. *Peace* (421) is an antiwar play in which a giant beetle draws Peace from a cavern where she has been imprisoned. *Lysistrata* (411) is also antiwar, and both it and *Thesmophoriazusae*, produced the same year, show women taking over. *Frogs* (405), another first-prize winner, is about the sad plight (in his view) of Athenian drama and literature generally, featuring Aeschylus, Euripides, and others.

Aristophanes' almost exact equivalent in English drama is Ben Jonson, whom we know learned from these old Greek plays. They deal with real as well as imaginary people, actual events, and current customs, usually presented in a grotesquely exaggerated form. He took on some very unpleasant and powerful people, such as Cleon, and it is amazing to me that he escaped prosecution, exile, or death: Perhaps he was lucky that Cleon, who certainly attacked him publicly, was killed in battle.

In 423 Aristophanes produced *Clouds*, an attack on Athenian sophists, intellectuals, and philosophers generally, with particular attention paid to Socrates, who is really the chief character. We have it only in a revised form, which was not produced, and what the original and actual production was like we do not know exactly. It played badly, and the play as we have it seems to me crude, implausible, and dull, though it can be, and has been, successfully produced in modern times. Like other Aristophanes works, it lends itself to ingenious direction. It bears no relation to the real Socrates and his views or the actual life he lived but presents him as a very unpleasant and wicked man. Why, then, did Plato in his *Symposium* present Socrates and Aristophanes as friends, and the latter as an attractive person? I can only suppose that Aristophanes knew Socrates only by malicious hearsay at the time he wrote *Clouds* and that his views changed dramatically once they met and talked. Socrates bore no grudge. He said of attacks on him in the theater: "If the criticism is just, I must try to reform myself. If it's untrue, it doesn't matter."

Aristophanes was deeply and strongly critical of Pericles in *Acharnians*. This was only to be expected in view of his personal opinions. For his evident hatred of war was created by the unhappiness, destruction, and slaughter that Pericles' imperialism and vainglory made inevitable. Behind its cultural achievements lay a presumption of Athens's right to control the Greek world, and that led inevitably to a struggle with Sparta that could only end in her destruction, or that of Athens. As Pericles himself said, Greece was not big enough for both. The Peloponnesian War, which was to settle, once and for all, which was to be the paramount Greek power, began in 431 B.C., and Pericles' famous oration was delivered the following year. That marked the acme of his influence. Thereafter it was downhill.

In 430 B.C., almost certainly as a direct result of the war, Athens was afflicted by the worst plague in her history. Thousands died. Pericles' own family was devastated. The plague broke the morale of Athens. It was seen as the punishment of the gods for their neglect by the Periclean power. It is true that their humanism came close to atheism in the minds of many. His favorite philosopher, Anaxagoras, was seen as impious for his cosmology and cosmogony. Phidias, his cultural commissar, was blamed for his depiction of human figures in the frieze of the Parthenon. Protagoras's dictum that "Man is the measure of all things" was held to be a plain declaration of disbelief in divinity. Thucydides, the historian of the regime, was already known for denying the gods any role in the march of great events. At the end of the plague year, the revulsion of popular feeling drove Pericles from office. He was tried for embezzlement of public funds and fined. The next spring, public opinion swung round again. He was once more elected *strategos* and tried to rebuild his position. But it seems he had caught the plague germs, which undermined his strength and now humbled his proud spirit. He died of it six months after being reelected, and men said it was a punishment. There was a witch hunt of his entourage. Phidias had been prosecuted for stealing public gold when making his giant statue of Athena. He was acquitted but was then arraigned for impiety and put in prison, where he died. Protagoras and Anaxagoras were likewise hounded, and enemies even indicted Pericles' mistress Aspasia (about whom more will be said), though she won acquittal. By 428 B.C., the brilliant group of humanists who had run and adorned Athens in the name of man had been broken up and dispersed.

Socrates survived the plague, something his friends noted with surprise. While many fled the city or kept to their houses, Socrates continued his usual practice of walking the streets and talking to all, regardless of possible contagion. The fact that he escaped was taken as a tribute to his generally healthy life and exercises. By now he was forty, a middle-aged man and becoming, in his own way, an Athenian celebrity. It is time for us to turn to his work and in particular his idiosyncratic methods of practicing philosophy.

IV

Socrates the
Philosophical Genius

The onset and ravages of the plague, the death of Pericles, the decline of his regime and the suspension of his cultural program, the prosecution of his leading followers, and the general malaise in Athens, had a personal effect on Socrates. They forced him to ponder seriously his function in life. He had always been a thinker and enjoyed talking and debating with fellow Athenians. But he had never had a job. Now he began to feel he had a mission. The age of Pericles had been admirable in many ways: It had encouraged architecture and building, painting and pottery, music and the theater, as well as manufacturing and commerce and the useful arts. But there was something missing. It was all very well to reiterate its slogan, "Man is the measure of all things," and to insist that human beings were not helpless playthings of the gods but masters of their fate. But what sort of a person was man? The Pericleans were eager to improve art and technology in all their aspects, and had to a great extent succeeded in doing so. But what about improving man?

Was it possible? And if so, how? It seemed to Socrates that these questions were never asked and ought to be asked.

It was not that clever and thoughtful Greeks were idle. On the contrary. They asked questions all the time. But they tended to concentrate on the world, and the distant worlds—or whatever they were—in the sky. The Greeks called it the cosmos, and enquiry centered on how it worked, cosmology, and how it was originally created, cosmogony. As a young man, Socrates engaged in such questioning himself. He inherited a considerable body of knowledge, or as he came to see, pseudo-knowledge. There were, for instance, a group of wise inquirers in Ionian Greece, to the east, especially in Miletus. Such were Thales, active around 580 B.C., over a century before Socrates, his pupil Anaximander, and *his* pupil Anaximenes. Thales, who was possibly a Hebrew, or Semitic, was later called by Aristotle the founder of the physical sciences. He used the Egyptian system of land measurement to invent the technique of geometry. He was said to have foretold the solar eclipse that occurred during the Battle of the Halys (May 28, 585 B.C.). He was a polymath who drew snatches of exact knowledge from the accumulated wisdom of the Semitic world, but his conjectures were eccentric. He believed, for instance, that magnets have souls. He thought the earth floated on water.

Anaximander wrote the first treatise on the cosmos, which has survived, though only in fragments. He conceived it as a unity, operating under laws, with the moon and the sun moving in cycles. He was the first to draw a map of the earth. He invented the gnomon for astronomic observation. Like Darwin, he believed that man and animals evolved. He answered the question, "If the earth rests on water, what supports the water?" by answering that it was not necessary because it lay at the center and at equal distance from everything, so was held in tension: everything is in conflict and tension, and this is the principle of universal stability, an argument often described as the first example of a priori reasoning in science. He was aware of the sheer size of things and introduced terms for "unlimited" and "the infinite." But his follower Anaximenes rejected the water explanation and substituted air, which when dense became fire or winds or clouds and was subject to condensation. Another Easterner, Heraclitus of Ephesus, expanded the tension theory, noting that this was exactly how the bow and the lyre worked, an example of the close observation and shrewd deductions of which these early Greek philosopher-scientists were capable. To him, the principle of tension was signified by the *logos*, the symbol of eternity. It was also transcendent wisdom and the elemental fire. He was of royal blood but gave over the throne to his brother so he could write his *Treatise*, dealing with the *logos*. A fragment reads:

> God is day and night, winter and summer, war and peace, plenty and famine, all the opposites which sustain things. Men are foolish creatures who must subject themselves to the logos or law. . . . The people must fight for the law, as for a defensive wall, for all human laws are nourished by the divine, which is one.

He also wrote: "We ought to grasp that war is common and natural, as is justice which is strife, that all things come about in accordance with strife and what must be." His best-known saying is "You cannot step twice into the same river." But what does it mean? In antiquity he was known as Heraclitus the Obscure. When Euripides gave Socrates his works, Socrates commented, "What I understand is splendid. What I do not understand may be good too. But it would take a deep-sea diver to get to the bottom of it."

On the other hand, there were the Greek seers who lived in what is now Italy and were later known as the Westerners. Parmenides and Zeno lived in Elea and were also called Eleatics. They were systematic arguers and were the first to produce the kind of consequential series of deductions that are still in use today in learned circles. Parmenides in particular invented and honed philosophic tools and reflected on the term *to be*—what can be known must be—and nothing else can be—all expressed in a poem set in hexameters, chunks of which survive. He was between fifty and sixty years older than Socrates. Democritus was Socrates' contemporary, and his theory that the universe was composed of infinitely small, undifferentiated pieces of matter, which he called atoms, and that their changing positions produce the visible compounds of the world identified by our senses still holds good, in part at least. His work was typical of the way in which the early Greeks identified portions of truth, tension and atomism, for example, but mixed them with speculative ideas we find nonsensical. Democritus, for example, thought the soul was composed of fine, round atoms and was as perishable as the body. Zeno was a superb arguer but thought that, properly speaking, there was no motion and no plurality.

The Greeks had the gift of seeing concrete substances in abstract terms—hence their mastery of geometry and their complex ideas about the universe, achievements certainly denied to the Egyptians and even, on the whole, to the Hebrews. The difficulty was that they possessed neither the instrumentation nor the knack of engaging in empirical investigations. They could observe, but they did not experiment, except by accident. Pythagoras began the systematic study of numbers and, among other innovations, introduced the number ten, and in due course his work became of incalculable value to science. But when Socrates was a young man and explored, as he later said, the limits of scientific knowledge, he could not see any way of pushing them further. The cosmos was mute. It could be seen but could not speak. Above all, it could not answer questions.

That, to Socrates, was the great objection to work on the external world. He was the Great Question Master. His deepest instinct was to interrogate. The dynamic impulse within him was to ask and then use the answer to frame another question. At an early age—in his twenties, most likely—he saw that science, or the investigation of the external world, was, for him at least, unprofitable. But the investigation of the internal world of man was something he could do and wanted to do. He had always been accustomed to walk the streets of Athens, to dawdle in the Agora, to take exercise in its suburban parks and gardens, and always to study the activities of people working in these places: tanners, metalworkers, shopkeepers, water sellers, hucksters, barrow folk, scribes (for in his day professional writers were just beginning to produce scrolls for sale), and money changers. Walking to Piraeus, the port, or in the countryside surrounding Athens, he observed sailors, farmers, horse trainers, and men and women working in vineyards, olive groves, and dairies. All these people had tongues in their heads, and he gradually discovered they were happy to use them. So he asked them questions, and they answered. Neighbors and colleagues joined in. There is abundant testimony that Socrates had charm. He got on with people of all kinds and classes, from lowest to highest. He joked. He smiled. He never got angry. He was polite. He made the people he questioned, and cross-questioned, feel important, and he seemed to find their answers valuable.

Once Socrates found he could do this, his reason told him that it was his work in life. And an inner voice confirmed this. People said, "You seem to have a gift for talking to people, Socrates, and getting their opinions. You ought to go in for public life, and stand for office." But his inner voice said no. It never told him what to do, but it was emphatic, he said, in telling him what *not* to do. It counseled strongly against a political career: "My voice and my reason," he said, "agreed against politics." Snatches of his sayings about his work have come down to us. "I believe God ordered me to live philosophizing, examining myself and others." "To practice philosophy has been indicated to me by God, through divination, dreams, and every other means by which divine orders have told anyone to do anything." Of the physical sciences, he remarked "I have no share in them." But philosophy was the theater of reason, and "I am the sort of person who is persuaded by nothing except those propositions which appear the best when I reason."

Socrates was not the only person practicing forms of philosophy in Athens. Far from it. There was a tribe of persons who engaged in intellectual instruction, some born in Athens but others itinerant, coming from all over Magna Graecia but tending to settle in Athens because there was more money there and more young men of high or wealthy birth to engage their services. These teachers were called Sophists. They charged high fees and some became rich. They taught a variety of skills but chiefly rhetoric or the art of persuasion, equally valuable in the law court or the council chamber or the Assembly. Some were more high-minded than others, but as a class, they were far from popular. Toward the end of the century, when things went badly for Athens, they were blamed for encouraging reckless young men to go into public life and equipping them with skills that enabled them to attract followers and so get the City into trouble. Aristophanes attacked them in *Clouds* before he got to know Socrates, and when he thought he was one of them, a mistake made by some others. But all those who actually knew Socrates, especially if they engaged in argument with him, realized that he was not a Sophist in any sense. In the first place, he never charged fees. He did not even engage to instruct anyone particularly in anything, and "he never gave a public lecture in his life." What he had to say he gave gratis, but in any case, as most of his time was spent asking questions, he could not easily be described as a tutor or teacher of any kind. Moreover, the last thing he wanted to impart was the basic stock-in-trade of the Sophists' worldly wisdom, how to "get on." What he taught, in so far as he consciously taught anything, was goodness. Aristotle, who knew all about Socrates' work from Plato, wrote: "Socrates occupied himself with ethics, and not at all with nature as a whole."

Far from teaching gilded youth how to dominate the Assembly or persuade Athenian voters to elect them *strategos*, Socrates liked to talk to people of all classes and occupations. He said, "I am a universalist," using a word just coming into common currency. Cicero, who had read Plato but who also had access to many works lost to us, summed up Socrates better than anyone else. "Socrates," he wrote, "was the first to call Philosophy down from the skies, and establish her in the towns, and introduce her into people's homes, and force her to investigate ordinary life, ethics, good and evil." To this Plutarch added: "He was the first person to demonstrate that life is open to philosophy, at all times, in every part, among all kinds of people, and in every experience and activity." Of course, as Socrates became known, affluent young men sought him out. He was invited to symposia or dinner parties, which inevitably were attended by the well-to-do. Plato, who knew Socrates during the last ten years or so of his life, when he was a celebrity of sorts and much sought after in rich homes, tends to overemphasize this side and stage of his life, just as Boswell does of Dr. Johnson's. In reading Plato's record of Socrates' dialogues, it is important to remember that Plato, an aristocrat on both sides of his family, did not share Socrates' spirit of democratic give-and-take and classlessness. It is important to imagine Socrates arguing with ship captains in Epirus, or market-gardeners in the suburbs or men who made swords and shields in the Athenian workshops.

Socrates went about Athens talking to people, mainly asking them questions, all his life. He was always interested in trades and occupations and how they were conducted, not least in trade secrets, as they were, and are, called. No doubt his questions always began with the man's or woman's duties and only gradually went on to more complex matters of beliefs and morals and opinions. Like Dr. Johnson, he was extremely interested in how things were done by experts. Craftsmanship fascinated him. He accumulated a good deal of information, like Dr. Johnson, concerning products and processes. We would call this knowledge. But Socrates did not. By *knowledge* he meant wisdom or insight, and he always disclaimed possessing any. He seems to have felt he knew nothing about the things that really mattered. When his friend Chaerephon, while visiting the Oracle of Delphi, asked if any man was wiser than Socrates, the answer came: "There is none." When told about this, Socrates was not flattered but puzzled. He eventually concluded that what the Oracle meant was that his wisdom consisted in knowing his own ignorance. Others, including the Sophists, had no more wisdom than he had but would not admit it. The oracular judgment had the effect of spurring him on to continue and extend his inquiries, and engage in them more seriously and systematically. In the *Theaetetus* Plato has Socrates—who obviously got the idea from his mother's work—compare himself to a midwife. He cannot teach Wisdom because he has none, and he cannot give birth to Wisdom any more than he can give birth to a child. But if someone else has Wisdom within him, or her, he can assist, by his questioning, and help them to give birth to the truth they carry within their minds and hearts.

Plato called this questioning *dialectic,* and went on to refine and develop it himself. The usual term is *elenchus,* the word for the questioning the barrister offered in court to extract information from a witness who might be reluctant to give or, more likely, did not even know he possessed. Socrates' approach to this process was ironic, a mode he invented or certainly popularized. Irony is one of the most difficult terms to define, but is almost in itself the measure of an advanced civilization: The fact that one of the best-known characters in mid-fifth-century-B.C. Athens habitually used it shows how far the Greeks had already moved in sophistication and subtlety. The *Oxford English Dictionary* defines irony as "A figure of speech in which the intended meaning is the opposite of that expressed by the words used; usually taking the form of sarcasm or ridicule in which laudatory expressions are used to imply condemnation or contempt." That is a fair try but actually less clear, and less succinct, than Dr. Johnson's *Dictionary*: "Mode of speech in which the meaning is contrary to the words." He was following Quintilian, the famous first-century-A.D. Roman teacher of rhetoric: "A figure of speech in which something contrary to what is *said* is to be *understood.*" Socrates was the only person he cited as a master of the art. Macaulay, in his essay on Bacon, suggests that to witness irony you should listen to the abuse exchanged in a London traffic jam: "A drayman, in a passion, calls out 'You are a pretty fellow,' without suspecting he is uttering irony." It is one of the fascinating facts about irony that it is often used instinctively by uneducated people unaware of their skill. That does not necessarily mean, unfortunately, that they recognize it when used by others. The great radical politician Aneurin Bevan once said to me, "Never use irony in politics. Whenever I have done so it has got me into trouble. A lot of your hearers always take you literally." He added, "It makes no difference how heavy your irony is, and how obvious it is to you. It is not obvious to them."

This was a warning Socrates might have done well to heed, for irony was a critical element in his eventual indictment and condemnation. But of course he would have taken no notice of the warning. Irony was inseparable from his intellectual personality, in public or in private. He could not function as an articulate human being without resorting to it, often. Its commonest form, in his case, was to say, "I am an ignorant fellow. I know nothing. That is why I ask so many questions." This was a disarming tactic, whether he was in the company of clever young aristocrats or Athenian workmen. They might detect an element of irony but they never knew how much, and in any case they took it as a compliment. It was a sure way of getting them to open up. However, although the tactic worked with some, it failed with others. Not that they took Socrates literally. Rather, they thought him deliberately deceptive. They saw the use of irony as low cunning. It is curious that Aristophanes, who used irony himself, unaware that Socrates had started the game, in *Clouds*, written before he met him, never shows him using irony, except as lying. Plato, in the *Republic*, shows Socrates violently attacked by Thrasymachus, the Sophist, for his "habitual shamming." He saw Socrates' irony as a clever cover for his quite genuine ignorance or confusion and his inability to give sincere answers to perfectly proper questions. Sometimes, too, the irony was censured as mock modesty. Thus in the *Gorgias* dialogue of Plato, there is this exchange with Callicles. *Socrates*: "Since by 'better,' you don't mean 'stronger,' tell me again what you mean. And teach me more gently, admirable man, so that I won't run away from your school." *Callicles*: 'You are mocking me."

Some people found Socrates' ironic tone puzzling simply because it was part of his apparently lighthearted approach, in which quite straightforward jests and fun played a part. Alcibiades refers to Socrates' "endless ironizing and jesting." There is a distinction here, but also a confusion. Socrates seems to have felt that another missing element in Periclean Athens was a sense of humor. Or rather, though the tragedies of the Big Three, and the comedies of Aristophanes (and others), presented the two sides of the human predicament, the distinction was too formal and absolute, as though the impresarios at the Theater of Dionysus were to say to the audience, "Today we are going to make you weep," or "Today we are giving you a good laugh." Whereas, Socrates felt, what was required was the ability, which he possessed, to slip deftly and almost imperceptibly from seriousness to laughter and back again—the essence of sophisticated communion.

Socrates' use of humor is perfectly illustrated by Elizabeth Bennet in Jane Austen's *Pride and Prejudice*: "I hope I never ridicule what is wise or good. But follies and nonsense, whims and inconsistencies do divert me, I own, and I laugh at them whenever I can." Socrates said almost exactly the same thing. He insisted, "I never jest at the sacred." But "all the mortal world" was fair game. And he switches from one mood to another without a noisy change of gear. The best way to grasp, and appreciate, Socrates' methods is to read the texts that have come down to us, especially the score of Socrates' dialogues recorded by Plato. They cannot give us the pleasure of listening to Socrates' voice, which was melodious, the essence of courtesy, patience, sensitivity, and calmness, but they do to some extent show how his mind worked, especially its combination of lighthearted flexibility and high seriousness.

He valued words, and the first thing he tried to instill was the need to use them with care. That meant defining them. Aristotle said Socrates was the first to make a point of definitions. What he liked was to take a subject—love, piety, friendship, reason, etc.—and ask someone to begin by defining it. Thus in *Laches* he tackles courage. Laches thinks this an easy one. "If anyone stands his place, and defends himself from the enemy and does not fly, he is courageous." Socrates agrees but then asks, "What about the Scythians, who fight just as furiously when they fly as when they are pursuing?" "Yes, but that is cavalry. I was talking about the heavy infantry of Greece, who do as I say, and are brave." "Except for the Spartans. At Plataea, they were not willing to remain and fight them, but fled. Then, when the Persians broke ranks, they rallied, and fought like cavalry, and thus won the battle." "True." "Of course," said Socrates, "you did not answer correctly because I did not put the question correctly. I should have made it much broader, asking about not only soldiers in battle, but sailors at sea and in storms, and those who show fortitude in sickness, poverty, in politics, against pain or fear—there are surely some men, Laches, who are brave in these things?" "Surely." "Try again, then, to tell me what exactly is that bravery which is the same in all these?" And so on. Socrates helps him by trying to define the element of swiftness common in running races, playing on the harp, speaking, and learning. Laches eventually tries to define bravery as "endurance of the soul." But Socrates and he agree that not every kind of endurance involves bravery. Laches also, prompted by Socrates, says that endurance existing in conjunction with what is prudent, admirable, and good, "is more likely to be a form of bravery. But what if bravery subsists with folly? Is not this hurtful and evil working? And can bravery, though seemingly admirable, coexist with folly? Is not what you are saying, that only prudent bravery can be truly admirable?" The dialogue continues, embracing medicine and the treatment of inflammation of the lungs, the estimation of numbers in deciding when to fight a battle, the relative bravery of men in cavalry combat who are experts on horses, and those who are not, the use and misuse of boldness, the kind of bravery needed to pursue an argument, such as this one. Socrates then brings in Nicias, who defines bravery as "the science relating to dread and daring, both in war and in all other things." Laches: "How absurdly he talks. . . . He is a trifler." Socrates: "Let us then teach, but not revile him." Then they get back to medicine, and on to agriculture, and the fear of dying, and prophecy, and many other matters. The discussion ends without conclusion or rancor but with an agreement to meet the next morning.

Laches is a characteristic early dialogue, in which Socrates, not Plato, is in charge and animating the whole. When you try to condense and epitomize such a work, you realize how hard it is to understand the dialogue as a whole—that is, presenting a discussion in readable and comprehensible form, which had probably taken place over many hours, perhaps days, and had often been confused, running off at a tangent, irrelevant or at times pointless, and all this without recording devices or, most probably, secretarial help. We must assume that Plato shortened many of the exchanges, and rationalized, clarified, and sharpened the contributions, including Socrates' own. The wonder is that he still emerges from these early discussions as a definite character and that his purpose in holding them can be grasped. Plato was a great artist, and at this stage in his career was still an artist aiming at verisimilitude.

What, then, was Socrates' purpose? It should be understood that there were in his day, have been ever since, and are likely to be in the future two fundamentally distinct kinds of philosophers. The first tells you *what* to think; the second, *how to think*. Socrates belongs to the second group, emphatically, though (as we have already seen and shall see again) he had opinions, too. He was interested in people, rather than ideas, and keenly anxious to discover how people think and whether they can be encouraged to think more clearly and usefully. His methods in cross-questioning his subjects demonstrate time and again what he is up to. He wants to show that on almost any topic—not least the big ones he tackles, like justice, friendship, courage, virtue as a whole—the received opinion is nearly always faulty and often wholly wrong. He asks a simple question, gets the usual answer, and then proceeds to show, using further questions springing from a vast reper-toire of occupations, history both human and natural, and literature, that the usual answer not only fails to fit all the contingencies implicit in the question but also contradicts analytical reason at its highest or even common sense at its lowest. Socrates was always suspicious of the obvious, and he can nearly always show that the obvious is untrue, and the truth is very rarely obvious. The way he does this is the substance of the discussion and gives it its excite-ment and dynamism. Reaching a conclusion is not the object. The object, rather, is teaching the people to whom he is talking how to think and, not least, how to think for themselves.

Each session, therefore, embodies a lesson, and the underlying assumption is that the lesson is learned only when the young men (or others) to whom he is talking can carry on in the same way, on other topics, when Socrates is not around to steer, coax, nag, bully, and guide them. What is particularly liberating about Socrates and is just as relevant today as in the fifth century B.C., is his hostility not just to the "right answer" as to the very idea of there being a right answer. He would have been particularly opposed to the modern system, used in every kind of bureaucratic form-filling and increasingly in examination papers at all levels of the education system, of asking people not to give *their* answers to a question, but to examine various answers and pick the *right* one. This denial of independent thought by individuals was exactly the kind of mentality he spent his life in resisting. Of course, by teaching people, especially young men (often from influential families) to think for themselves, Socrates was treading a dangerous path. Athens (for most of the time) was a democracy of sorts and a free, certainly a liberal, society. But its institutions rested on consensus and to some degree were precarious, especially if the consensus was not forthcoming.

It was one thing to have the Assembly swayed by rhetoric. Allowance could be made for that. But if each citizen thought for himself, was taught to distrust the received wisdom and even to reject the notion of a correct answer to problems, then getting the consensus, especially the right consensus, would prove to be hard, if not impossible. In my view, this was a powerful consideration, which led to criticism of Socrates' activities among the young and, in a time of crisis, to his prosecution, conviction, and death.

But we will come to all that later. What is worth observing now is that, even in the early dialogues, when Plato is producing the real, actual, and historic Socrates and recording accurately what he said, the thought was stirring in his mind that there were dangers in teaching clever young men to be intellectually independent. Perhaps already, even when listening to Socrates talk or when first setting it down, there was stirring in Plato's mind the idea of his *Republic*, the utopian state that would be immune to such threats because it was protected from rash and impetuous thinking by a powerful consensus of guardians.

We can be in absolutely no doubt that Socrates would have disliked and disapproved of the republic Plato wanted to bring into being. Indeed the two men were very different in almost every respect, and it is one of the great paradoxes of history that they came together, the one to found, the other to record, the beginning of true philosophy. In youth, Plato hero-worshipped Socrates; in his maturity, he repudiated him without appearing to do so to the inattentive reader or perhaps without knowing himself what exactly he was doing. Socrates, to begin with, was a conservative radical, while Plato was a radical conservative. Socrates was open to any idea that could leap over the various barriers of logical proof that formed a racecourse in his mind. He was conservative in that he respected old customs concerning gods and heroes and others cherished by the public, for he did not wish to put ordinary people off the essential truths by a foolish desire to demolish inessential myths. He was a conservative radical precisely because he was a moderate, genial, sensitive, and generous human being. Plato, on the other hand, was inclined to transform natural conservative instincts, which sprang from the empirical wisdom of ordinary people, into a specific ideology, which inevitably moved from a humane traditionalism into absolutist dogma. It is no wonder that Karl Popper, in his *The Open Society and Its Enemies,* identified Plato as the ultimate progenitor of the twentieth-century totalitarian state, even though this argument is open to serious objections. I suspect that if Socrates had been able to read the *Republic* and to assess its influence through the twentieth century, he might have been even more severe than Popper.

That there was a widening bifurcation between Socrates and Plato is one of the most obvious facts in the history of philosophy. Exactly when it occurred in the Platonic oeuvre and which dialogues can be described as Socratic or mainly Socratic or mainly Platonic or wholly Platonic has been debated by scholars for generations. I prefer a broad-brush approach that makes a general contrast between the Socratic and Platonic mentalities and then counsels the reader to study the dialogues and make up his or her own mind. This, I think, would be the Socratic approach.

Well, then: Socrates was a sensible, practical, down-to-earth man, interested in usefulness, not perfection, and inclined to make allowances for the infinite variety of human nature. He was not a poet but a master of spoken prose. Plato was a poet. Worse, a frustrated poet. He was in parts of his being a visionary, a mystic, a transcendentalist. He believed in the transmigration of souls. He thought the soul was a repository of inherent knowledge, which could be rediscovered. He believed in transcendent forms as opposed to individual objects. Socrates believed in none of these notions.

The great Socrates scholar Gregory Vlastos, who has,

in my opinion, written the best book on the subject, *Socrates: Ironist and Moral Philosopher* (Cambridge, reprinted 1997), has listed ten key ways in which the real Socrates differed from the artificial creation labeled Socrates who increasingly figures in Plato's works. First, Socrates is exclusively a moral philosopher. Second, Socrates does not believe at all in "forms" or "recollections of knowledge." Third, Socrates insists he has no knowledge/wisdom and goes on seeking it eclectically. Fourth, Socrates has no complicated, tripartite notion of the soul, composed of rationality, passion, and cravings. Socrates takes a simple view of the soul, immortal and unified, which Christians share. Fifth, Socrates is not interested in mathematical sciences, except where they are obviously essential, as in land surveying, and neither possesses nor claims any scientific expertise. Sixth, his view of philosophy is populist. Seventh, he has no political theory as such. He is often critical of the way Athens is run and its manner of doing things, but he prefers it and its laws to those of any other state. Eighth, he rejects homosexual love except at a superficial level. Ninth, Socrates sees piety as service to a rigorously ethical deity, and his personal religion is practical, expressed in action. Finally his philosophical method is to pursue truth by refuting propositions he induces his interlocutors to put forward: He never departs from this strategy, and when he is presented as doing so, he is not Socrates but a hybrid creature I call Platsoc.

On the other hand, the fact that in the course of the dialogues and other writings of Plato, Socrates the man is gradually replaced by Platsoc, or Socrates the ventriloquist's dummy, should not prevent anyone interested in what Socrates really thought from reading the entire corpus. In many places Socrates and Plato are inextricably intermingled. For instance, in the dialogue *Gorgias*, named after a famous Sophist from Leontini in Sicily, Socrates asks Gorgias to define what he specialized in teaching, rhetoric. Gorgias was notorious for saying a well-trained rhetorician or legal pleader could find plausible arguments to support any case, however flimsy, in law or politics. He himself taught pupils to speak in short, almost symmetrical phrases, and to balance theses and antitheses in a kind of pulsating rhythm, to play on words and to have audible echoes in the course of a plea. In short, he made a speech seem and sometimes sound like a piece of music. He took great pride in his skills and had some of the style and arrogance we associate today with a highly successful and ingenious advertising executive. He answers Socrates by saying rhetoric is one of the key human activities because the essence of a successful public leader or statesman is not so much knowing what is to be done as the ability to persuade people to do it. You can tell a first-class orator by his gift of getting people to do something even if it is manifestly unjust. Gorgias then retires, being replaced by his pupil Polus, and Socrates then uses his cross-examination technique to get Polus to agree with a proposition that Gorgias would certainly have rejected: that it is better to suffer injustice than to inflict it, and that if one has done a wicked thing it is better for you yourself, as well as for everyone else and society, to be punished than not to be punished. This is not the doll; it is genuine Socrates. Indeed, it is quintessential Socrates.

Polus, having been argued into repudiating his master's lifework, is then replaced by a man called Callicles, who produces a variation on Gorgias's amoralism. Virtue, he says, and therefore happiness, are to be found essentially in self-will, for those with the skill and willpower to exercise it, and this is so whether what is willed is just or unjust. Callicles is voicing a doctrine later to be laid down powerfully by Nietzsche, who was fascinated by the Socratic dialogues—especially when Plato was in charge—and had illuminating things to say about them. Socrates does not actually refute this outrageous proposition but concentrates instead on drawing the distinction between Callicles' life of action and his own life of philosophy, with an overwhelming preference for the latter: "An unexamined life is a life not worth living." This last observation is essential Socrates, too, and occurs in different ways elsewhere in his discourse. But, that apart, Socrates is fading and morphing into Platsoc. He contrasts philosophy with the activities of Pericles, Miltiades, and Cimon, denouncing them with a vehemence that is alien to Socrates. The underlying proposition, that the true philosopher does more for the citizens of Athens by encouraging them to become virtuous than by leading them into victories and conquests, may be Socratic, but the context in which the point is made and the passion injected into the argument are ugly and un-Socratic: Platsoc again. Moreover the dialogue ends with a mythical presentation of the soul being judged after death, which is obviously Plato himself speaking.

Gorgias, then, illustrates the huge problem of extracting the real views of Socrates from the labyrinthine entanglements in which Plato—by intention or by the irresistible compulsion of his own powerful spirit, we cannot judge—has confusingly embedded them. It is rather like what happens today when a media democracy goes to war. Indeed the same word is used. Correspondents are "embedded" in active service units, and what they transmit to their TV stations and newspapers is a mixture, sometimes a confusing and contradictory one, of their own views and observations, and what their military mentors, or guardians, wish them to transmit. But at least they can, if pushed too far, protest, even if it means being sent home. Socrates was the innocent victim of Plato's embedment—which often involved a Procrustean bed, too—and never, of course, knew how his brilliant pupil would use him after his death.

All the same, it is clear what Socrates the real man thought about some important issues, and we can present them plainly. We have seen how he taught. Now we must look at—not so much what he taught, for he had no system and, strictly speaking, taught nothing in the way of dogma—but at what he believed.

V

Socrates and Justice

When the great economist John Maynard Keynes was asked what made a successful capitalist, he replied "Animal spirits, mainly." This observation applies to Socrates too. There was about him a vigor or animation of mind, a power of cheerfulness, vivacity, and liveliness. Some vital power or energy seemed to flow into and out of him. By "animal spirits," there is no implication of boisterous irresponsibility, such as we find in an overactive child. Rather, a zest for life and a desire to convey it, by revving up the minds of those with whom he came into contact. And in certain contexts the zest could become formidable. I can well believe the image of him striding across the field of combat, in hoplite armor, carrying his weapons, with the Spartans shrewdly deciding to leave him strictly alone: They sensed a zest for combat they could do without. Socrates compared himself to a gadfly, stinging the massive Athenian horse of state, an elderly cart horse or battle-scarred charger, out of its complacency or comatose inertia.

In conversation, too, the zest could be formidable. One of his young friends, Alcibiades, compared him to an electric ray, whose bite induced a sense of numb helplessness. But there is a danger this remark may give a wrong impression. Socrates did not exactly *bite* in argument; he rarely if ever snapped. His practice of philosophy could be defined as "reflection on propositions emerging from unreflective thought." It is worth repeating his saying "A life without examination is not worth living." But his examinations, or cross-examinations, were courteous, even genial. A person might think afterward that he had made a fool of himself in dialogue with Socrates, but he is unlikely to have felt that he had been deliberately led into folly. Socrates clearly liked people, the great majority of them anyway.

His philanthropy, or love of his fellow men, was quite unlike the conscious humanism of Pericles and his associates. There was no taint of atheism about it. Socrates was too aware of human weakness and shortcomings to think men could ever substitute themselves for divinity. Socrates believed in God. It was precisely because he believed in God that he devoted his life to philosophy, which to him was about the human desire to carry out divine purposes. He believed he had a command to do this and that by wandering around Athens and talking to people—"examining" them—and examining himself, he was doing as God told him. When accusations were later brought against him, he was charged not with atheism but "not believing in the gods Athenians believed in." This had perhaps an element of truth in it. Socrates did not believe in the traditional pantheon of Greek religion, with gods specializing in particular services and leading tumultuous lives that were more mythology or fiction than serious religion. When Socrates was at his most devout, he always refers to "god" or "the god," not "the gods." He was a monotheist.

Of course Socrates, being a courteous and sensitive man, always deferred to the superstitions of the common people—or the elites, for that matter. He had no wish to offend. He often used the vernacular of popular religion. His famous last words, "We owe a cock to Asclepius," are an example. Being a practical man, an empiric, he thought popular religion was at worst harmless, at best a calming and ordering factor in society. It was also a consolation to people who led hard and often harsh lives of privation. He was no Richard Dawkins, eager to disabuse the common herd of their illusions in the name of triumphalist rationality. But Socrates, a moderate in all things, always knew when to draw the line. He did not go so far as Pericles, who openly dismissed superstition in public affairs. But having been a soldier, he believed diviners and soothsayers should be kept out of military decisions. One of his friends was the general Nicias, who should have evacuated his army from the plain of Syracuse on August 27, 413 B.C. He was persuaded by a lunar eclipse to remain for the requisite ritual days and lost everything, as Thucydides relates. Socrates hailed Nicias's courage in the *Laches* dialogue on the subject. But he also says in it that the diviners must obey the general, not the other way around. He would have advised Nicias to withdraw as fast as he could and so save his army.

The role of religion in public affairs, however, was not Socrates' principal concern. What he sought was ways in which he could help individual men and women to become better morally. This was the mission God had given him in life, as he truly and even passionately believed. He seems to have felt close to God, in some ways. God communicated with him through a *daemon,* or spiritual voice, which told him not to do certain unwise things, like become a politician. But if Socrates was a monotheist in essentials, with a strong sense of a personal god, he did not, I think, believe God to be omnipotent, as the Hebrews did. The Greeks in general imposed limitations on divine power. To them, the gap between gods and men was often narrow and could be bridged, by apotheosis, for instance. Their heroic mortals often behaved like gods, and their gods like mortals, exhibiting jealousy, cruelty, and other base emotions. Socrates would have none of this nonsense. He had a careful doctrine of what Leibniz was later to call theodicy, a vindication of the divine attributes, especially justice and holiness, in respect to the existence of evil. He felt no difficulty in the attempt "to justify the ways of God to men." But he did it by rejecting the notion of divine omnipotence. In book 2 of the *Republic* (not a text where, in general, the real Socrates speaks, though I think he does in this particular passage) he remarks, "So God cannot be the cause of all things but only of good things. Of evil things he is not the cause." In saying this, Socrates was rejecting many events and possibilities dear to the Greek mind. But he was also rejecting, for instance, the kind of dramas described in the Book of Job, a text he would have found of the greatest interest though not, in the end, plausible. But there is no sign that Socrates believed in a kind of dualism or Manichaeanism. He left the problem of evil open and concentrated on the good.

Socrates spent much of his time pondering the Good Life and how to attain it. For he believed, and it was the core of his belief, that only by striving to lead good lives did humans attain a degree of content in their existence and happiness in eternity. He had a simple view of the body and the soul and their relationship. The body was the active, physical, earthly aspect of a person and was mortal.

The soul was the spiritual aspect and was immortal. The body was greedy for pleasure and material satisfactions, was selfish, and if not kept under control, became a seat of vice. The soul was the intellectual and moral side of the person, which had a natural propensity to do right and to improve itself. It could be, with proper training, the seat of virtue. The most important occupation of a human being was to subdue his bodily instincts and train himself to respond to the teachings of the soul. This training took the form of recognizing, understanding, and learning about virtues and applying this knowledge to the everyday situations of life. Such, to Socrates, was the essence of wisdom. Knowledge, virtue, and wisdom were thus intimately related, and exploring these connections was the object of his "examinations," of himself and others.

In his personal life, Socrates did everything he could to subdue his bodily cravings. He ate and drank sparingly, even though he attended dinner parties for the sake of friendship. He declined to pursue a lucrative career, like the Sophists, so kept his needs to a minimum. He had no shoes. He wore few clothes. He was content with simple shelter. He declined an offer of freehold land on which to build a house. He had little or no ready cash, though he was pleased to see the rise of a bookselling trade in Athens and reported you could buy new manuscripts there cheaply. There were always friends to help him when he was in real need, which was rare. "I can do without." "There are so few things I really want." The great thing was to keep fit and well. A sick man with no money is bound to be a burden. But he was never sick and was perfectly fit when he died at age seventy. With the body under control, and everyone testified to that, he was in a position to cultivate his soul by pursuing virtue. He is said to have remarked, "I have never knowingly harmed any man, or sinned against God." That sounds like boasting, and Socrates was the last man to boast. But it was almost certainly true.

What is also true is that Socrates' notions of the body and the soul and of their relationship became, in time, standard. Before his day, the word *psyche* had existed, had indeed been in use for perhaps a millennium, but meant something quite different and nebulous. In Homer, souls are rather like ghosts and disappear if we try to touch them. They are doppelgangers of the dead and live in Hades on the asphodel meadow. This was probably how most people in Socrates' day saw the soul, if they thought about it. Within a generation or two of Socrates' death, however, his idea of the soul—in all its powerful simplicity, unlike the complex and precarious soul of Plato—had been accepted by a wide range of intelligent, educated Greeks. It fitted in perfectly with Christ's teaching and so passed into the moral conceptions of Christianity and has been the received concept of the soul ever since among civilized people. If you and I say "soul," we mean what Socrates meant, and he gave it that meaning.

That was a remarkable contribution to the moral furniture of our minds. But it was not the only one. Socrates took an optimistic view of human nature. He believed that the great majority of people wished to do well and that wrongdoing was usually the result of ignorance or false teaching. Once a person knew the truth, his instinct was to do what is right. Hence knowledge led directly to virtue, in Socrates' view. This underlined the importance of education, especially the kind revealed by his examination technique, which was designed to show the individual that he possessed far less knowledge than he thought he did, and thus to encourage him to acquire more.

One vital subject on which knowledge was particularly lacking was justice. All Greeks favored justice. Very few, if any, knew what it was. Worse, Socrates found that what many thought was justice was, in fact, the opposite. If there was one topic on which Greek knowledge of virtue was fundamentally defective, it was justice. Aristotle was right to stress Socrates' importance in revealing the need for definition of terms, for it is when you begin to study definitions accurately that you start plumbing the depth of ignorance, especially about justice.

In the first book of the *Republic*, Socrates, who is still himself at this point, disputes with the Sophist Thrasymachus the answer to the question "What is justice?" Thrasymachus answers, "Justice is the interest of the stronger." In every society, the rules defining what is just and unjust, he says, are determined by the ruling elite, the strongest section of society, in its own interests. Socrates does not accept this, but he does not give his own answer, and book 1 ends inconclusively. In book 2, he ceases to be himself and becomes Platsoc. But what we gather, in this and other places, is that Socrates thinks each issue should be judged on its merits and that the virtuous man has no difficulty in distinguishing between justice and injustice. What he does make plain, again and again, and in the strongest possible language, is that doing justly comes before any other consideration. It is better, he says, to suffer anything, even death, rather than act unjustly. He says in the *Apology*: "If a man is worth anything, he would give no weight whatsoever to any other consideration—even life itself— rather than act unjustly. All that matters, when he acts, is whether his action is just or unjust, the action of a good or an evil man." That Socrates' emphasis on the paramountcy of acting justly was widely adopted is shown by the emphatic statement of Isocrates in *Panathenaicus*, two generations later: "Victories won in violation of justice are more despicable than are morally righteous defeats."

It is evident that justice in the abstract did not concern Socrates. What did concern him, always, was action in practice. One common Greek view in his day, as Thrasymachus implied, was that justice was usually a form of self-interest. Asked, "What is a just man?" a Greek would reply, "A man who does good by his friends, and does evil to his enemies." Socrates would not have this. "A just man is one who does good by his friends, certainly, but also does good to those who have harmed him, thereby seeking to convert an enemy into a friend." This view appears in several versions, the theme always being to return evil with good. We are close here to Christ's advice to "turn the other cheek." Socrates says plainly in *Crito*, "It is never right to do wrong, or to requite wrong with wrong, or when we suffer evil to defend ourselves by doing evil in return." It is this clear view that marks the point at which Socrates turns his back on moral relativism, in any guise or circumstances, and opts firmly for moral absolutism. If you know a thing is wrong, never do it, ever.

This rule led Socrates to cross another historic moral watershed and to repudiate absolutely one of the deepest-rooted maxims of Greek behavior, both by individuals and states—the law of retaliation. Of course retaliation was not peculiar to Greece. It is common to most if not all societies emerging from savagery and tribalism and feeling their way to civilized modes. In the Hebrew Book of Exodus, immediately after chapter 20, in which God gives Moses and the Israelites the Ten Commandments—which seem to have stood the test of time in many if not most societies—there follows a chapter laying down the law of retaliation, in the case of a woman with child, hurt in a struggle, in drastic fashion (Exodus 21:23–25): "And if any mischief follow, then thou shalt give life for life, eye for eye, tooth for tooth, hand for hand, foot for foot, burning for burning, wound for wound, stripe for stripe." We do not know when the Book of Exodus was compiled, but one theory is around 700 B.C., which would make the compiler a contemporary of the Greek poet Hesiod, second only to Homer as a moral mentor. Hesiod goes further than Exodus: "If an enemy starts it, saying or doing something harmful to you, you must certainly pay him back twice over." That is more vengeful than the Hebrew sage, who only demands one eye for an eye, not both: That would be wrong.

Socrates set his face against the entire theory and practice of retaliation. In the *Crito* he lays down the five principles of his command. We should never do injustice.

Therefore we should never return an injustice. We should never do evil to anyone. Therefore we should never return evil for evil. To do evil to a human being is no different from acting unjustly. Socrates was fully aware of the momentous nature of his rejection of traditional Greek morality and justice. For immediately after announcing his five principles, he adds that "few are those who believe or will believe this. And between those who do and those who don't there can be no common ground. Each feels contempt for the other."

Socrates' stand was taken up at a time when the issue of retaliation as a public policy was of vivid and immediate importance. In 431 B.C. Euripides set the scene with his *Medea*. Socrates was almost certainly in the audience. This horrifying play is a tale of revenge in the name of justice. What Medea does is totally out of proportion to what she has suffered, and it may be that Euripides is making the point that, if retaliation (or revenge) is accepted as a principle of justice, it is extremely difficult in practice to ensure that the retribution corresponds to the offense. Medea says she is exacting "just repayment with God's help," but admits afterward that she "has dared to do a most impious deed." The word impious is significant, for it conveys the implication that the whole notion of "just revenge" may be impious. We know that Socrates helped Euripides with at least one of his plays—"patched it up." It is possible that he persuaded the poet to insert this line in *Medea*.

Then, four years later, the whole question came up in the most startling fashion in the real world of war and politics. Athens had to decide what to do about Mytilene, the chief city of the island of Lesbos, which had rebelled against Athens. It had now been occupied by Athenian troops. The question of punishment came before the Athenian Assembly. Such cities were often shown no mercy in the heat of war. Both Sparta and Athens could be ruthless in exacting what they saw as justice. In four cases—Histiaea, Melos, Scione, and Torone—what we would call genocide occurred. But these massacres were carried out by army commanders acting on their own authority. In 427 B.C., the decision was taken by the democratic Assembly of a constitutional state, after full debate. Thanks to the oratory of the demagogue Cleon, a proposal was passed ordering the commander to execute without trial all adult males in Mytilene and to sell into slavery all women and children.

This motion of extermination, or genocide, carried democratically after argument, is unique in Greek history or, so far as I know, in any history. It clearly pleased the majority. But it must have shocked a minority, including Socrates, who I assume was present. I like to feel—indeed,

I am pretty certain—that he played a part in what followed. After the vote, Cleon had immediately dispatched a ship to Mytilene to take the Assembly's decision to the commanding general with instructions to carry it out before the Assembly had second thoughts. But it *did* have second thoughts. After a night of anxious discussion among the moderates, in which I assume Socrates took part, their leader, Diodotus, appealed to the Assembly the next day to reverse their decision. His arguments were for the most part practical. It was the oligarchy at Mytilene, he said, that had ordered the rebellion, not the demos. Most of the people were on the side of Athens and had forced the city's surrender to the Athenian troops who now occupied it. To punish them, alongside the oligarchs was obviously wrong, for the oligarchs were guilty, whereas the demos was innocent, indeed on Athens's side. This injustice would be noted among all Athens's allies and colonies. Diodotus says, "I think it better for the empire to allow ourselves to suffer wrong than to destroy, however justly, those whom we ought not to destroy." The last phrase reveals a Socratean thought peering out among the general argument of expediency, and it persuades me that Diodotus allowed himself to be guided by the philosopher, in part at least. He does not go so far as to repudiate the principle of retaliation as justice: He wanted to win the vote. He did so. The decision was reversed, and a fast trireme was dispatched immediately to Mytilene to rescind the instructions to the general. Happily, it arrived in time, and the honor of Athens and its people was saved.

Here we have an episode when the views of Socrates were applied immediately in public action, rather than slowly becoming consensual over generations. And there is strong reason to believe that his personal intervention was decisive in securing this outcome. His voice from God might forbid him to become a politician, but it did not inhibit him from seeking to influence political decisions in the name of true justice, as opposed to the false justice that was the norm of Greek society in the mid-fifth century B.C.

Socrates' rejection of retaliation was the most important practical event of his philosophical life. It was also one of the most important events in the history of philosophy. The best discussion of it is chapter 7 in Gregory Vlastos's *Socrates* (which I strongly advise readers to peruse, if they have the time). What Socrates argued is extraordinarily uncompromising. It is moral absolutism at its most stringent. He is saying in effect: If something you do wrongs somebody else and, a fortiori, large numbers of people, it is so bad in itself, and so bad for you, that nothing of good which it achieves can compensate for the evil. It may win a victory or even a war; it may bring you everything you value, joy, comfort, security, and long life; it may arouse the approval of those you love, your family and friends; it may be necessary, as you think, for their self-preservation and your own; but if it is wrong, then you must not do it. Even if it would win the whole world, you must not do it. Your life itself would not be worth living if you can preserve it only by wronging others.

This is a hard doctrine, and it is not surprising that the world in the last two and a half millennia has often, even usually, found it too hard to follow, even while accepting it in principle. There is some evidence that Plato found it hard, and abundant references show that Aristotle could not quite swallow it. He felt that revenge was a constant impulse in human nature, as ineradicable as the anger that prompted it. Indeed, he defined anger as "the desire to inflict retaliatory distress." The absolutely fundamental moral truth that a wrong done to me gives me no right whatever to inflict the same wrong on the doer was a little too much for Aristotle to take. In fact, Socrates was the only Greek to grasp and fully accept the moral axiom that retaliation, or revenge, or whatever we choose to call it, is wrong and must never be accepted or defended. He was the first to articulate the axiom, and to insist upon it *contra mundum*.

Since Socrates first laid down, or discovered, this new

moral law—God's law, as opposed to man's law—it has been broken countless times, by statesmen and generals and democracies, let alone dictatorships and absolute monarchs, as well as by countless individual men and women in their personal dealings. If we examine World War II, for instance, we are forced to admit that the self-righteous democracies, Britain and the United States, in pursuing what they reasonably argued was a just war, against infamous enemies, on occasions—some might say often—yielded to the temptation of retaliation. Yet they recognized that it was a temptation, and that what they did was open to criticism. Even at the time, and certainly on many occasions since, the rightness of the bombing of Germany and Japan and the use of the atomic bomb has been debated endlessly. The fact that these debates took place at all is due to the initial moral revelation of Socrates and its subsequent illumination of the universal conscience.

There was another aspect of justice to which Socrates devoted attention and produced new insights: the position of women and men's attitude to them. Now Socrates had important things to say about women, which again marked a historic turning point, but before we come to them, it is convenient to clear out of the way the question of homosexuality in ancient Greece and the extent to which it was fashionable and involved Socrates. In the late seventh and sixth centuries B.C. a large number of Attic black and red figure cups were inscribed "[a boy] is beautiful," and one or two vessels that have survived even show men and boys engaged in anal intercourse. In the second half of the fifth century B.C., however, such visual evidence of the practice declined and by Socrates' death was rare.

The practice was largely confined to the landowning and wealthy families whose young, well-dowered virgins, once they became nubile, were strictly segregated. It was hard, up to the mid-fifth century B.C., for a young man of good family to find himself alone with a young woman, and romantic lovemaking in upper-class circles was difficult if not impossible. Instead, young men formed romantic friendships with older men, exchanging their good looks for instruction, wisdom, guidance, and patronage. These liaisons were further promoted by the formal sports and exercise of the elite, in which men were naked, by the institution of the *symposium*, or all-male dinner party, and by warfare, with its stress on courage, friendship, and glamorous display. But it is doubtful if many of these friendships took a physical form. Male prostitutes, we know, were held in detestation, and males who enjoyed the passive role in sodomy were despised by Greeks of all classes. There was a good deal of talk about the beauty of male youth, however, and this found itself reflected in literature, including the works of Plato.

Socrates spent his life in argument with men (chiefly), not least young men, and regularly attended *symposia*. Inevitably, then, he has been said to have had sexual relations with men or at least to have tolerated homosexuality among his society friends. In my reading of the relevant texts, I find no evidence that Socrates ever engaged in homosexual lovemaking. He certainly agreed that a boy or young man might be beautiful. But Socratic love for males was limited to eye and mind contact. The endless talk of passion between males at *symposia* he put up with in rather the same way he accepted popular polytheism and superstition. But when he participated in it his tone was jocular. There is an important passage in Plato where a speech by Lysias, a metic (immigrant second-class citizen), son of a rich shield maker, who himself became wealthy by speechwriting, is analyzed. In it, Lysias says a youth should grant his favor to a man who is *not* in love with him rather than to one who is. Socrates treats it as a joke: "Splendid! I would have walked to Megara and back to hear such a speech!" Then he says, "I wish Lysias would add that a youth should grant his favors to a poor man rather than to a rich man, to an elderly man rather than to a young man and, in general, to ordinary people like myself. What an attractive democratic thing that would be!"

Elsewhere, in the *Phaedrus* for example, when a piece of writing is held up for admiration, Socrates objects to the notion of love as chiefly a matter of physical desire. There seems to be a wide difference between Plato's mature notion of the word *eros* and Socrates'. For Plato, eros can generate an intoxicating force, a kind of madness. Socrates' eros is measured, moderate, lighthearted, genial, jocular, and sane. Again, Plato rejects sexual bliss because it defeats the attempt to separate the soul from the body (part of his absurd notion of the complex soul), and therefore, though allowing body contact between males, he forbids "terminal gratification." Socrates has no objections to orgasm, but will allow it only between male and female. Pederastic lovemaking of any physical kind, but especially leading to orgasm, he thinks bad for both boy and man. He calls it "devouring." He utters a key passage in Xenophon's *Symposium*: "The man reserves the pleasure for himself, the most shameful things for the boy. . . . The boy does not share, like a woman, the delight of sex with a man, but looks on sober at another's intoxication."

A clearer example of Socrates' view of homosexuality, as distinct from benevolent male friendship, comes in Plato's *Symposium*, when Alcibiades arrives at the dinner drunk, and seeing Socrates there, makes a long and embarrassingly frank speech about his relationship with the seer. Among other things, he gives a detailed description of his unsuccessful attempt to seduce Socrates. Alcibiades in his youth was a person of exceptional beauty and allure, as all accounts agree, who had no difficulty in making himself irresistible to any older man who had a taste for boys. What he wanted from Socrates, whom he admired enormously as a fount of wisdom, was an intimate relationship, in which he would exchange the delights of his body in return for Socrates giving him the delights of his mind. Socrates would have none of it. He rejected Alcibiades' advances, which took various forms, indeed not with harshness but courteously and with rational arguments. At last Alcibiades contrived an occasion when Socrates was obliged to sleep at his house, and "when the lamp was put out and the servants had retired, I felt I must be open with him and cast aside all doubt." So he shook Socrates to make sure he was awake and explained his intentions without any possible ambiguity: his beauty for Socrates' brains. Socrates tried to argue him out of it, but Alcibiades persisted:

And so, wishing to hear no more from him in words, I got up, and threw my coat about his body. I then slipped under his threadbare cloak (it was winter, and cold) and put my arms about him. There I lay the entire night, holding this superhuman genius tightly. . . . But, despite all my efforts, he showed himself completely above all my solicitations. I felt him to be disdainful and superior and almost contemptuous of my beauty—though he was perfectly polite—and his virtue had a kind of courteous but proud rejection of my body thus laid before him. Nothing whatever happened, and I eventually fell asleep. When I awoke—let all the gods and goddesses be my witness—I was still as unviolated as if I had slept with my father or an elder brother.

This passage may strike a modern reader as surprising. While it shows that Socrates was not inclined to homosexuality, it also shows him passively acquiescent in the face of Alcibiades' advances. There was no rejection because Socrates saw only too well that his failure to respond would be a grievous injury to Alcibiades' pride. Anything more would have been unbearably brutal. His passivity was exact and well judged.

We can now turn to his relationships with women and his view of their function in society. The evidence is not very plentiful, but what there is proves exceptionally interesting. During the *Symposium*, as described by Plato, the conversation turns to love, and Socrates introduces the character of Diotima of Mantinea, a city in Arcadia. He says, "She was my instructress in the art of love, and I shall try to repeat to you what she said to me." He says she was "a woman wise in this and many other kinds of knowledge." He also says that she advised the Athenians on the way in which they should offer sacrifice to prevent the plague, which was spreading over Greece, from coming to Athens, and as a result of her efforts, it was delayed ten years. She seems, then, to have been some kind of priestess.

There follow, in Plato's account, several thousand words of dialogue between Diotima and Socrates, the woman taking the lead and Socrates submitting. Much of the substance, on the nature of love, is pure Plato, with his "forms" and his peculiar view of the soul and the "recovery" of knowledge. It need not concern us here, merely illustrating his irritating habit of foisting his personal views on others, in this instance Diotima as well as Socrates. There are, however, three aspects of this section of the *Symposium* that strike us forcibly. First, this is the only time Socrates tells us directly about his education and how he was taught by this remarkable woman. There has been much speculation about who influenced him as a young man and shaped his approach to philosophy. But here we are actually given a glimpse of his training, and it is fascinating to learn that his teacher was female—most unusual in the Athens of the fifth century B.C. Second, Diotima uses what we have come to call the Socratic method of questioning, with Socrates, in this instance, on the receiving end. She "examines" him. Now it is true that she then goes on to teach and impart knowledge in a way Socrates himself usually avoids, so that the discussion of love reaches a conclusion. All the same, it is striking that Socrates was introduced to his examination technique by a woman. He extended and refined it, but he did not entirely invent it. Diotima was thus more important in creating the Socrates we know than any other human being.

Third, there is a remarkable passage in Diotima's account of love concerning childbirth: its suffering, its glory, and its beauty. There is nothing quite like it in the whole of Greek literature. It leads me to suppose that his mother, the midwife Phaenarete, played a part in his relationship with Diotima. Perhaps she was responsible for introducing them. It is possible, indeed I feel quite likely, that Diotima, too, had experience of midwifery. The two women may have consulted together over a difficult case or worked in concert. This is the only time when we can fairly speculate about the part one of Socrates' parents played in his intellectual upbringing.

The second woman who played a part in Socrates' life was even more remarkable. Aspasia came from Miletus, the most southerly of the large cities Greek colonists built on the coast of what is now Turkey. Her origins were lowly but probably not slave class. However she is usually described as a hetaera, the term used for a mistress or woman in an irregular relationship with a man, one class higher than a prostitute. Hetaerae were usually aliens or slaves or freed women. They had some legal rights and paid a tax but rarely enjoyed full citizenship in Athens. They were often musicians or dancers or flute players hired to perform at all-male dinner parties.

Aspasia was exceptional in that she was a highly literate, well-read woman, who became a member of Pericles' circle and, five years after he divorced his wife, became his consort and remained so until his death. She clearly knew Socrates well, having met him on his peregrinations through Athens and, I surmise, having been "examined" by him. He had a high opinion of her intellect and literary accomplishments; when asked by the parents of a young man to recommend a master to teach him rhetoric, he mentioned Aspasia. This caused astonishment, but his advice was taken and proved sound. She taught other young men and helped Pericles with his speeches. Indeed, she might be regarded as the first professional speechwriter in history, and it is odd that this role should have been initiated by a woman. Whether she wrote all of his famous funeral oration, however, is doubtful, for it contains a disobliging reference to women: He said the woman in best repute is one who "contrives never to have her name mentioned, either in praise or blame."

Aspasia was popularly believed to be a power behind Pericles' throne and was attacked in plays and skits, most notably by Aristophanes in his comedy *Acharnians*, which won the first prize in 425 B.C. So she had in common with Socrates the enmity of this bitter playwright, though it is likely that, as with Socrates, he did not know her at the time of his assault. She seems to have been envied and resented in theatrical circles, for some years earlier, when Pericles was still alive, she was publicly prosecuted for impiety by the actor Hermippus. Pericles defended her with great skill and passion, and she was acquitted. After his death in 429, she took up with the politician Lysicles, but he was killed the following year. Her association with Pericles might not have gotten her into the history books, but her friendship with Socrates and his obvious admiration for her did. She figures not only in Plato but in Aeschines and Antisthenes.

Socrates was much influenced by these two brilliant women, so much so that he argued that women ought to play a much bigger role in Athenian society, and in particular ought to be prepared for it by receiving as full an education as males. He thought the elevation of women from their lowly status a matter of simple justice. As it was, they were under relentless pressure never to go out, never to acquire accomplishments, and never to lead a life of culture and pleasure, being simple household drudges and sex slaves. Even high-class women were expected to spin, weave, and make clothes. In Athens, unlike Sparta, where their status and rights were considerable, they could not as a rule own or dispose of property or sue in the courts, except for divorce. This may well have been in accord with Dr. Johnson's dictum that "Nature has given women such power that the law, rightly, gives them little," for Greek writers discoursed endlessly on the wiles of women and the tremendous and often disastrous effects of their sex appeal. Socrates thought that women were just as intelligent as men, ought to be educated accordingly, and should occupy responsible positions in society. The only constraint on their activity ought to be lack of physical strength. He believed they should be taught to ride and might even be trained as warriors if they wished.

Socrates' views on women are reflected in Plato's *Re-*

public, where he is shown advocating their education, training, and holding of official posts. Some of the guardians, the rulers of Plato's ideal state, are to be women. Unfortunately, Plato goes far beyond Socrates in rearranging society and the lives of women. He advocates, in effect, the abolition of the family for a community of wives and children, a proposition that Socrates would have laughed to scorn and that Plato himself came to repudiate in his later work, *Laws*.

What Socrates really wanted was no more than a system that allowed women to develop their minds and skills and realize their potentials. He liked to think of them leading responsible and fulfilled lives, but he had no objections to their confining themselves to looking after their husbands and children, if that is what they wished. But if they desired to run for office, even for *strategos*, let them. He trusted them. An Athenian custom he found repellent was the rule that an upper-class woman never went out unless accompanied by a slave, usually a male one. This was partly for her protection but also so that the slave might report back to his master if the wife did anything strange or reprehensible.

That brings us to the question of slavery. Among the inhabitants of Athens, about half were not eligible for citizenship: debt bondsmen, unfree (enslaved indigenous

treated as property

populations), *metics* or aliens, and chattel slaves. Slaves performed various jobs, especially those involving service to a master, such as working in a bank. Greek citizens, especially in Athens, were reluctant to work for another, believing this compromised their independence and amounted to a form of slavery. So slaves had opportunities to prosper, and that is how Pasion became the richest banker in Greece and also a free man. But for most slaves, born in servitude or battle captives, there was little chance of freedom, and in the colony of Ephesus in Asia Minor, there was a busy slave market to which they might be sent by an indigent master.

Slavery was an obvious affront to justice, as Socrates understood it. It is therefore strange that our sources do not show him opposing it, recommending its abolition, or even commenting on its existence. Perhaps there is a missing dialogue, which was "suppressed" by subsequent generations simply by the failure to have it copied—the fate of many works society found insupportable. Once again, we bitterly regret Socrates' decision to write nothing. His failure to examine slavery is the greatest lacuna in his otherwise comprehensive view of justice, indeed in his entire philosophy. Given his influence after his death, a sharp and reasoned condemnation of slavery would have had incalculable consequences, and perhaps have led to the abolition of this scourge of humanity many centuries ago. Of course it is possible that Socrates habitually questioned the justice of slavery in his conversations. I think it possible, indeed quite likely. If so, the implied rejection of slavery, like the explicit rejection of retaliation, would have played a part in the hostility to Socrates among some Athenians that led to his prosecution, conviction, and death. To these events we now turn.

VI

The Demoralization of
Athens and the Death
of Socrates

ocrates lived in a relatively open society, Athens, and was able to pursue his quest for wisdom and virtue and "examine" young and old, rich and poor, for the best part of half a century in complete freedom. There is no record of the authorities trying to inhibit his teaching or philosophizing at the time, though what he taught, especially on the subject of justice and wrongdoing, was often contrary to the Athenian consensus, and must have shocked the right-thinking. Nevertheless, his career as a teacher was not without its dangers. Athens was the most successful of the Greek city-states in terms of creating wealth, art, and ideas. For much of the fifth century B.C., it was the cultural capital of the civilized world. But because of its success, it was a hazardous place, both for politicians and for those who lived by their intellects. Intense competition generated artistic and cerebral innovation on a scale never before seen in history, but also envy, spite, personal jealousies, and vendettas. These were most notable among the elite but the citizens as a whole were notoriously volatile, critical of their leaders and all prominent persons, easily swayed, and vengeful toward those who failed in public enterprises or angered them by what they conceived as arrogance or pretension. It was a celebrity society in which celebrities could be torn to pieces as well as exalted. In some ways it was like New York, "the quintessential fast-track city," as Richard Nixon called it. In Athens, success was intoxicating but failure heavily punished.

Moreover, during the last phase of Socrates' life, Athens was a demoralized place that could suddenly turn ugly. In the Acropolis and the Agora, there was the strong if intermittent scent of the witch hunt. The sunlit years of the Periclean ascendancy never returned. Darkness fell with the great plague of 430 B.C., which killed most of Pericles' own family and eventually him. The plague destroyed the city's once peerless self-confidence. It appeared to be a judgment on Athenian hubris. It also decimated the ranks of the elite, destroying some of its ablest members. It had a perceptible effect on Athens's military and naval manpower, making it far more difficult to replace battle losses. The days when Athens's population was perceptibly growing were over. The plague reduced it by a quarter. There was little sign of recovery in Socrates' lifetime.

No leader was found with the dynamic energy and vision to replace Pericles, none with the consistency of purpose to wage successfully the Peloponnesian War (431–404 B.C.) he had undertaken. Leadership fell into volatile and irresponsible hands. First came Cleon, the brutal demagogue, who in 422 invaded Thrace but, after some initial successes, was defeated and slain at Amphipolis. There were periodic truces and long pauses when both Sparta and Athens licked their wounds. Then Alcibiades, Socrates' friend and would-be lover, came to the helm. He was not so much a demagogue as an adventurer, whose ultimate loyalty was to himself. In 416–415 B.C., he vociferously supported a grandiose plan to send a naval and military expedition to Sicily to subdue Sparta's important ally, Syracuse. The plan was opposed by the general Nicias (470–413 B.C.), who had emerged as a moderate in opposition to Cleon and was generally in favor of peace. But the plan was adopted nevertheless, and both Nicias and Alcibiades appointed to command, an unwise arrangement, to put it mildly. The expedition was large and splendidly equipped—"the most magnificent ever dispatched from Athens," according to Thucydides. Socrates watched the preparations with misgivings. He was never a pacifist and had fought heroically for Athens in his day, but he thought war was usually unwise and the struggle to the death with Sparta suicidal for Greece, as indeed it proved. The fact that both Alcibiades and Nicias were friends of his made his position difficult.

In the event Alcibiades was soon recalled to Athens to face charges of polluting the Eleusinian Mysteries, the most important of the private cults at Athens. This was typical of the riotous, drunken behavior in which he and his rich friends indulged. No contemporary writer tells us what exactly Alcibiades and his gang did or why they did it, and the whole business is as much a puzzle to me as the mysteries themselves. Fearing conviction and execution, Alcibiades then deserted Athens and went to Sparta to give advice on how they could destroy the expedition he himself had advocated, planned, and commanded. But he soon quarreled with the Spartans, too, and thereafter oscillated between the two sides in the war until he was murdered in Phrygia in 404 B.C. As he never failed to boast about his relationship with Socrates, and what he had learned from him, he was a serious embarrassment—and a danger—to the old philosopher, now in his middle sixties.

Nicias, too, proved an embarrassment, for in action he was an indecisive general, given to trusting soothsayers and diviners rather than his own military instincts. Despite reinforcements, the Sicilian expedition ended in total disaster, the soldiers slaughtered or left to starve to death in the quarries outside Syracuse, and the commanders, in-

cluding Nicias, executed. It was the greatest military de-
bacle in the entire history of Athens, an unmitigated defeat
redeemed only by the magnificent prose in which Thucydides relates it.

The war dragged on, Athens making valiant but increasingly desperate, even despairing, efforts to rebuild a
navy, to ensure food supplies, and to prevent the Spartans
from destroying what was left of her empire. In 406 B.C.,
an Athenian fleet won the victory of Arginusae, so called
after the islets between the major island of Lesbos and the
mainland of Asia. This was an important success for the
beleaguered city, but it was frittered away by the Athenian
politicians. The losses on both sides had been heavy. The
Spartan fleet was destroyed, but Athens lost twenty-five
ships and over four thousand mariners. Instead of congrat-
ulating the commanders on their success, the politicians
decided to indict the naval commanders for culpable neg-
ligence in not doing enough to save the lives of their men.
The prosecution was outrageous in itself, but it was further marred by two irregularities. First, the politicians
proceeded by a process in which the verdict was reached
not by a sworn jury but by a simple vote in the Assembly
of citizens. This made it the equivalent of the notorious
Bill of Attainder process which, in late Plantagenet and
Tudor England, cost so many innocent men and women

their heads. Second, the Assembly was forbidden to try the eight accused commanders individually but was told to judge them collectively by a single vote. This was against one of the central principles of Athenian jurisprudence and was plainly unlawful.

Socrates, as it happened, was directly involved in this scandalous proceeding. Though declining politics, he always did his constitutional duty as a law-abiding citizen, and this involved serving from time to time in the Senate of Five Hundred, and on this occasion on the committee of procedure, or *prytanes*, which decided the agenda for the Assembly. The committee, no doubt prompted by Socrates, protested the illegality and unconstitutionality of the proceedings. But the prosecuting politicians, backed by a mob formed by the families of the dead sailors, bullied the committee members, threatening to add their names to the indictment and so have them condemned and executed. One by one, the committee members gave way. Socrates alone continued to protest and refused to play any part in a legal farce that in effect was mob law. This took courage, and he was lucky to escape with his life. All the commanders were condemned en bloc, and six were promptly executed (two had escaped). In this desecration of Athenian justice, Socrates alone had upheld the rule of law.

Three years later, he again took a solitary stand against
moral and legal anarchy. Athenian reverses resumed after
the fleeting victory of Arginusae; the brutal, arrogant, but
highly efficient Spartan commander, Lysander, proved in-
vincible on both land and sea. In 405 B.C., he destroyed
what remained of the Athenian navy at Aegospotami and
blockaded the port of Piraeus, starving the Athenians and
forcing them to capitulate in the spring of 404 B.C. As was
his practice in taking over Athenian colonies and allies, he
suspended the existing democratic constitution of Athens,
replacing it by what we would call a junta of oligarchic
aristocrats. This was led by Critias, a man well known to
Socrates and first cousin to Plato's mother. In concert with
Theramenes, who led the more moderate antidemocrats,
he asked Lysander, whose troops now occupied the Acropolis, for help. Lysander forced the Assembly to suspend the
constitution, draw up a new one, and appoint a body of
Thirty Tyrants to rule the city. The Thirty, with Critias at
their head, seized dictatorial power. They appointed a new
executive under their control, set up a board of ten to rule
Piraeus, removed democrats from all offices, and began a
reign of terror against their enemies, personal and political. Theramenes begged Critias to appoint a new Assembly to give the regime legitimacy, and a list of 3,000 citizens
was drawn up but never published. In the end, Critias ex-

ecuted Theramenes, together with an estimated 1,500 other prominent opponents. Others were exiled, and most of the remainder fled.

Thus Athens acquired a Vichy-style regime, sustained in power by the Spartan troops in the Acropolis, playing the role of the Nazis. Socrates was obviously unhappy about it all. Not only was Critias his former pupil, but so was Charmides, one of his chief associates, the brother of Plato's mother. However, once the executions began, he denounced them publicly as unjust and unlawful. According to Xenophon, he was summoned before the Thirty and told to cease conversing with the young men immediately. He refused and was dismissed by Critias with threats. Critias might have had him executed. But his tactic, rather, was to get Socrates involved in the acts of the regime and to share its moral responsibilities. Socrates was instructed, with four other citizens, to seize a wealthy man, Leon of Salamis, confiscate his property, then kill him. The four obeyed, and Leon was, in fact, murdered. Socrates refused to have any part in this atrocity and simply went home. He expected to be arrested there and executed in his turn. He might have fled from Athens like so many others, but nothing would persuade him to leave his beloved city. It was now near the end of the year, and events turned against Critias. He had been unable to establish his authority over Piraeus, where many armed democrats had gathered. He went down there in person to see what he could do and was killed in a battle with the exiles under Thrasybulus. His associates were now deposed by the moderates, who negotiated terms with the democrats. The democratic system was restored in the summer of 403 B.C., and the rump of the Tyrants fled to Eleusis, where they were massacred three years later.

Thus ended this woeful episode in Greek history, leaving Socrates desolate and shaken but with his honor intact. He was, however, in some ways a marked man, being associated with three politicians who in these years of Athenian failure and disgrace had been credited by the citizenry with much of the blame for it—Alcibiades, Critias, and Charmides. All three figure largely in Plato's writings about Socrates, and Charmides had a dialogue named after him: He it was whom Socrates, unusually, encouraged to enter politics, and this was known. I think it unlikely that Critias, who was only nine years younger than Socrates, had been a pupil of his in the usual sense, but all three had come under his influence, and this was certainly known too. Now all three were dead, but none had been punished, strictly speaking, under Athenian law, after due process. So justice was unsatisfied. We must remember that about 1,500 Athenians had been judicially murdered or simply slain without any kind of trial, and their families and dependents were clamoring for revenge. Who was to be thrown to them? What about Socrates? Was he not the man who had argued against revenge as justice? And said that retaliation was wrong? All the more reason why he should suffer now.

One of the defects of the Athenian system of justice was that no clear distinction was made between the public and private interest in seeking the prosecution of wrongdoers. The state could, and did, prosecute. But so could private individuals, on behalf of the public. And they frequently did so. The law did not differentiate between a public crime and a private tort (wrong) as in England and the United States. Nor were there separate courts to underline the difference between public and private motivations in seeking legal redress. If, in the case of Socrates, matters had been left to the state authorities, it is most probable that he would have been left alone. The state had enough to do without taking on an old man in his late sixties. There had been revolution and counter-revolution in the law no less than in the Athenian polity. When the democrats returned to power, one of their first acts was to appoint a commission to revise and codify the entire body of law, which had been left in confusion by the Thirty Tyrants and their Spartan masters. It did not finish its work until the year 400 B.C. There were many private suits pending, launched by the families of the murdered victims, to recover their confiscated property. The courts were crammed with angry and frustrated litigants.

But there were in Athens men who conceived it their moral duty to punish Socrates or at least force him to leave Athens. One such was Anytus, a wealthy democrat who claimed he was acting from the highest motives in prosecuting Socrates. Plato, in *Meno*, calls him a well-bred man. But he was not well educated. He did not distinguish between Socrates and the Sophists, and his hatred of Sophists was passionate. In all likelihood, his mind on this topic had been shaped by Aristophanes' *Clouds*, which not only presents Socrates as a Sophist but accuses him of disgraceful and dishonest behavior. It is an instance of the dangers of unbridled and mendacious "satire." Anytus was not exactly the model of upright probity he claimed to be. He had been a general who in 409 B.C. had failed to prevent the loss of Pylos. He was threatened with prosecution but escaped by bribery. Perhaps for this reason he did not constitute himself the principal prosecutor.

Though he financed the case, Anytus left its public presentation largely to a youngish man called Meletus. He was a religious fanatic, fond of using the crime of "impiety" as a stick to beat public figures he felt were lacking in right-thinking religious zeal. He had been involved in the prosecution of Andocides, an associate of Alcibiades in the Eleusinian Mysteries affair. His speech on this occasion has survived and would do credit to a Southern Baptist fundamentalist from Arkansas. A third party was joined to this private prosecution, a man called Lycon, about whom we know nothing except Socrates' assertion he was a "professional orator." In sum, the trio who took it upon themselves to accuse Socrates were an unimpressive collection of near nonentities. The charge, as given by Diogenes Laertius, who may have transcribed the court document still preserved in the second century A.D., was as follows:

Meletus, son of Meletus, of the deme of Pitthus, indicts Socrates, son of Sophroniscus, of the deme Alopecae, on his oath, as follows. Socrates is guilty, first, of not worshipping the gods whom the state worships, but introducing new and unfamiliar religious practices; and, second, of corrupting the young. The prosecutor demands the death penalty.

This prosecution, though we may judge it outrageous, should not be deemed unusual in fifth-century-B.C. Athens. Very few prominent citizens who achieved a high profile in war or politics or business escaped an entanglement with the law. Many of them paid with their lives. Here are some of the famous or infamous who were brought to book, in one way or another, and my list is far from complete.

Cleisthenes, usually regarded as the creator of Athenian democracy, was prosecuted and exiled by his rival, Isagoras. He made a comeback, but his last years are a blank, presumably because he was thrown out again. Cimon, an immensely successful Athenian statesman and general as well as a promoter of public works, was prosecuted for bribery but acquitted. Two years later he was successfully ostracized, and after four years in exile, he had to beg to be allowed back in his native city. Pericles was prosecuted and tried for embezzlement and fraud. Aristes, the founder of the highly successful Delian League, was banished in 483 B.C. Themistocles, another highly successful Athenian statesman, was ostracized and exiled in 471. More ostraca bear his name than that of any other (presumably) unpopular Athenian. But he in turn successfully used the law against Hipparchus, Megacles, Xanthippus, and Aristides. Of Pericles' circle, the artist-architect Phidias was accused of impiety and of stealing ivory in decorating the Parthenon. He died in prison. Anaxagoras was also accused of impiety and took refuge in Lampedusa. Protagoras was twice in trouble with politically inspired prosecution. Aspasia, too, was prosecuted, but acquitted. The dramatist and poet Sophocles was prosecuted, also for impiety. So was Euripides. Pericles' son by Aspasia, also called Pericles, was put to death after the battle of Arginusae in 406 B.C. Among other prominent Athenians who met violent ends was the statesman Ephialtes, murdered in 461 B.C.; the demagogue Cleon, killed at Amphipolis; Critias, who was twice exiled and died fighting; Alcibiades, who was assassinated; and Nicias, though in his case his execution was ordered by Athens's Syracusan enemies. Persecution of the learned was by no means confined to Athens. Pythagoras was obliged to flee for his life from Samos to Croton, and later had to retire to Metapontum. Nor did it cease with the fifth century B.C. Aristotle had a charge of impiety brought against him and went into voluntary exile, "not wishing that Athens should commit a second crime against philosophy."

The first crime, of course, was the trial, conviction, and death of Socrates. We have a full account, not of the whole trial, alas, but of his defense, of what happened afterward, and of his death, and for once we can trust our sources.

The trial and death of Socrates constitute one of the great moral events of antiquity, indeed of history, and although in some ways they are recorded with an amplitude unusual for ancient times, nevertheless our information is profoundly unsatisfying. It is a thousand pities that Thucydides was not still alive to give us a thoughtful, continuous, accurate, and penetrating account of the event. Instead, we have four books of Plato, written with his customary artistry—indeed, in his description of Socrates' last hours, with surpassing genius—but with his usual combination of truth and transference (of his thoughts to Socrates) and his irritating *déformation professionelle*, the tendency to put ideas before persons. What is lacking is any general description of the trial and what Plato thought of it.

The first book is a dialogue, *Euthyphro*, set before the trial, in which Socrates, suddenly becoming aware that he is shortly to be tried for impiety, realizes that he is not quite sure what impiety is, or piety for that matter, and seeks definitions. As usual, he is frustrated by his own methods of examination, and all he shows is the muddle and confusion that arise when humans, anxious to appease or gratify the gods by offering sacrifices, are unable to explain the practical value of these pious actions or why the gods should want them. Socrates was by instinct and reason a monotheist and could perfectly well have argued that a human soul does indeed please an omnipotent god by offering him a pure and virtuous life on earth, and that this is the only form of sacrifice (which involves dispensing with carnal pleasures and all forms of self-indulgence) that matters. But to argue on this line would merely give hostages to his legal opponents, so he does not take it.

There follows the *Apology*, a supposedly verbatim recollection of Socrates' defense at his trial. Plato was present, so we must presume that the speech is, in general, accurately given. It also includes Socrates' remarks after he was convicted by a small majority and his response to the sentence of death by putting forward, as was his legal right, an alternative punishment. Third comes a dialogue, in jail, with one of his closest friends, Crito, who is anxious to provide funds so that Socrates can escape the death sentence and live in exile for a time. It gives Socrates reasons for declining the offer and his determination to uphold the dignity and sovereignty of Athenian law by submitting to it. Finally there is a description of Socrates' last hours, which includes an argument about the immortality of the soul and the nature of death. This is followed by his taking the penitential poison and his passing into the next world. Plato was not present but knew those who were, and his account has the ring, indeed the muffled thunder, of truth.

The absence of an account by Thucydides, that matchless analyst of motivation and historical settings, means that some aspects of Socrates' end will forever remain enigmatic. The trial took place in the late spring or early summer of 399 B.C., when Athens was still shaken by the cruel and bloody events during the tyranny of the Thirty, the Quisling government made possible by the Spartan victory and occupation. The 1,500 prominent citizens killed under this ferocious regime formed a significant percentage of the entire male citizenry of Athens and a much higher proportion of those actively involved in public life. Although by the time of the trial the democracy and the rule of law had been restored for three years, the courts were still clogged with litigation arising out of the drastic events under the Thirty, including property confiscations, and the loss and restoration of citizenship rights. It is amazing that, in the circumstances, such a prosecution, which many must have seen as frivolous, was allowed to proceed. Unfortunately there was no attorney general in the Athenian democracy. In England and the United States, this official, the chief law officer of the state, has the right to veto a legal process he judges contrary to the public interest. Likewise, in an Athenian court, there was no presiding judge who after hearing the prosecution case, can, in England and America, throw out the case as unjustified, frivolous, or incoherent. Any investigation of the Socrates case is bound to reveal the Athenian legal system as profoundly flawed.

That may well have been Socrates' view too. But his position throughout was that, as an Athenian citizen, he was fully subject to the laws and bound to abide by them. On many occasions he said, "I am grateful to God for making me a man, as opposed to a woman, a Greek as opposed to a barbarian, and an Athenian as opposed to a foreigner." His love of Athens was boundless, and the value he attached to the privilege of being free to walk its streets and talk and argue with its people was the spring of his life and all its motions. He could not be without it, and therefore never considered exile. Athens to Socrates was life.

Socrates, then, accepted his trial as a perfectly valid expression of Athenian law and democracy. Many expected him to disappear before it could take place, and go abroad. But that to him was unthinkable. He did not make any preparations. He consulted nobody learned in the law and engaged no one to speak for him. His old rhetorical mentor, Diotima, was dead. Aspasia, that other friend and expert on persuasive rhetoric, may still have been alive, if elderly, but there is no evidence she was still part of Socrates' life. He took no counsel that we know of. We have to accept that Socrates was a curious mixture of genuine humility and obstinate pride. He never made claims for himself as to knowledge or virtue. On the other hand, believing in justice as he did, he would not be unjust to himself. He believed he had a mission from God to examine and improve people. No power on earth, no threat to take away his freedom or his life, would deflect him from pursuing that God-ordained purpose.

The circumstances of his trial were unfavorable to him. He had to speak, in the open, to a jury of 500 members, enlarged by a crowd of onlookers composed of his friends and the merely curious, those with nothing better to do. One of the most difficult things we have to do, in the early twenty-first century, is to transport ourselves back 2,500 years, to a city of not many more than 150,000 people, with huge cultural and political pretensions but in many ways with the narrow outlook of a medium-size provincial town. Most Athenians knew one another, at least by sight. That knowledge was flavored by gossip, rumor, superstition, and prejudice. Most people in Athens had heard of Socrates, and many had seen him pottering about. He was thought to be "clever." Now as Socrates himself remarked on more than one occasion, Athenians did not like people merely because they were clever. It was a term, if not exactly of abuse, at least of suspicion. So Socrates was clever, was he? Then why does he wander about, with no shoes, almost in rags? Something wrong there, eh?

In physical terms, we have to try to imagine Socrates addressing a town meeting in the Midwest in the third quarter of the nineteenth century. The issue was capital, in that the man's life was theoretically at stake, but probably nothing would come of it. In other respects, it was a routine affair, nothing special. Socrates was used to talking, but always to small gatherings. He did not have a seasoned orator's powerful voice. I have spoken to gatherings of five hundred or more in various parts of the world and had no problems. But then I have always had amplification. Socrates had nothing but his voice. He was not speaking, either, in the theater at Epidaurus, with its superb acoustics, but merely in an uncomfortable open space in a dusty corner of the Acropolis.

His audience would have been roughly of three parts. One third knew him, had actually met and talked to him, knew the kind of things he said—and what he did not say—and felt there was no harm in him. They would have voted to acquit him without much regard for the procedures in court. Another third of the jury also knew him or of him, but at one remove. They had seen or knew of Aristophanes' play about him, *Clouds*, first performed twenty-five years before, but probably revived from time to time. Its hostility and lies created lasting prejudice against Socrates as a nuisance and troublemaker. Very clever: oh yes, very clever indeed. There had been other theatrical attacks on him, including an entire comic play, whose text has disappeared. Such mud sticks, and plenty of mud had been thrown in Socrates' direction over many years. A third portion of the jury, in any likelihood, had no views at all about Socrates. But they probably disliked him, as being "clever," or reputedly so. And why was he of such importance as to occupy the attention of the court, when there was so much more of genuine importance to be dealt with? These people would not have listened hard, and in any case it was clearly not too easy to hear everything that he said: He complained several times of interruptions.

Nor was the substance of Socrates' defense calculated to win over either those prejudiced against him or to attract the indifferent. His strongest argumentative virtue, a sinuous and sinewy subtlety, could not work with a mass audience. His habitual flavor of irony was a positive handicap. His best strategy, and one that a professional advocate would certainly have recommended, was to bring forward a succession of witnesses of impeccable character to testify, first, to his observance of the outward forms of Athenian religion and, second, to his having instructed them in ways that had led to their strong affection for virtuous civic principles. This would not have been difficult to do. But Socrates would not do it. It was against his principles in that it gave a misleading view of what he had been trying to do in his life for the best part of half a century.

He was not in the least interested in the outward observance of religion, but in its inner content. Nor did he instruct young men—or old ones, either—in civic virtue or
in anything else. His object was to help, not teach, by his
examining method—teach people to think for themselves.

Socrates' attempt to explain to his dull Athenian mass
jury what he was trying to do was dangerous in two ways.
First, it involved telling them about his inner voice from
God, which ordained him to conduct philosophy as he understood it. This in itself was sufficient proof he was not an
atheist as such. His cross-examination of Meletus elicited
that the young fanatic did indeed accuse him of atheism,
and to that extent the first part of the indictment was re-
futed. But the jurors were probably not much interested by
this point. What did impress them, and far from favorably,
was Socrates' claim to be guided by a special divine command. Ordinary people who have had no such experience
do not like to hear about those who claim to have a private
line to the divinity. They scent presumption and arrogance. They feel that such persons are liable to make public nuisances of themselves, especially if, as Socrates
appeared to be saying in his defense, this special divine
voice gave him commands that took precedence over any
others, including, presumably, the standing orders of the
civic deities. Here, indeed, Socrates appeared to be con-

firming the indictment, that he had substituted new gods, or god, one specially devoted to him, for the traditional gods of Athens.

Second, and worse, Socrates insisted on resurrecting the old tale of the prophetess of Delphi, who declared that there was no one in Athens wiser than Socrates. Some of the jurors would already have heard it. Others had not. Both groups might have been, and probably were, shocked that Socrates would bring it up in the context of his trial. Again, it smacked of arrogance and insensitivity. Of course, to those of us who have been able to follow the full flow of Socrates' thought, thanks to Plato, his object in referring to the oracle is clear and even admirable. It was central to his whole philosophy. At least he was aware of his own poverty of knowledge. In describing to the Athenian jurors his attempts to explore the minds of his fellow Athenians to discover, whether they possessed any wisdom and whether they were conscious of possessing none, he was in fact trying to defend the reputation for truth of the god who inspired the prophetess. He concluded that she was, after all, speaking the truth, for his admission of being ignorant, of *knowing* he had no wisdom, made him unique in Athens, and to that extent, in confessing and acknowledging his miserable bereftness, wiser than his fellow Athenians, who thought themselves to know more than they did. But the subtlety and irony of this argument was quite beyond most of his hearers, who probably thought that Socrates was merely finding a new and tortuous way of praising himself. It was all very clear, no doubt, and to hell with him! So he was the wisest man in Athens, was he? Well: an Athenian jury would show what they made of *that* claim.

Some of Socrates' friends, listening to his defense, must have winced when he thus played into his enemies' hands by his candor, and by the fact that he clothed it in that most dangerous of all vestures, irony. However, when all is said about the inadequacies of Socrates' defense, what probably led to the guilty verdict had nothing to do with it. The damning points were the two names: Critias and Alcibiades. Both were hated figures. Alcibiades had been rich, handsome, reckless, full of braggadocio and temerity, proud as the devil, hugely appealing, and infinitely wicked. He had Athens at his feet and then led it into the most disastrous military adventure in the whole of its long history. In his wicked and childish way, he had blasphemed the most sacred of Athens's private religious cults, the Eleusinian Mysteries, and condemned accordingly, he had fled to the Spartans, turned traitor to Athens, and advised her enemies how to attack her successfully. Forgiven and reinstated, he had achieved some successes, but met failure, too, and was again a suspect exile when the Persians, conspiring with the Spartans, had him murdered.

Critias, born in 460 B.C., was ten years older than Alcibiades, and a follower and associate of his in some of his exploits, both antireligious and political. He was a writer, poet, and dramatist, some of whose works, which have since disappeared, were once attributed to Euripides. Whereas Alcibiades was by inclination a democrat and populist, Critias was an elitist who valued his aristocratic connections, and on the surrender of Athens in 404, he returned as a violent supporter of the pro-Spartan Thirty Tyrants and took a prominent role in their atrocities. In Xenophon's account, he was the leader of the extremists among the Thirty, and in a desperate attempt to prolong the regime, he was killed fighting the democrats in the spring of 403.

In 399 B.C., Alcibiades and Critias were the two most hated names in Athens. But they were both dead, and nothing further could be done by Athenians to avenge themselves upon them. Moreover, though associates of both, and especially Critias, were still alive and at liberty, they were covered by an act of amnesty that Anytus and other moderate democrats had caused to be passed in 403 B.C. in an attempt to heal wounds and reunite the shattered political consensus of their city. It was probably because of the inhibiting role of the amnesty that Anytus was under pressure from his side to find a suitable guilt victim who could be blamed for the sins of Critias and Alcibiades and punished accordingly. Hence his decision to attack Socrates and finance his prosecution.

Socrates had taken no part in the events of 404–403 B.C. and thus was not covered by the amnesty. What he had done, many years before, or so it was widely believed, was to teach both Critias and Alcibiades, introducing them to impious and immoral ideas of the kind attributed to him in Aristophanes' *Clouds* or worse, and sowing the seeds of wickedness that eventually produced the evil fruit of treason and mass murder. This, I am sure, was the line of thinking that led directly to the prosecution of Socrates. Whether either of the two hate figures was ever his pupil in any regular sense is doubtful. But they had been at times on friendly terms with him, and Alcibiades had openly boasted of his admiration for Socrates and his wisdom. Critias had family connections with Plato, now Socrates' favorite pupil, and it could easily be shown, or at least was widely believed, that Critias and Socrates had remained friends.

Here we come to another fatal consequence of Socrates' unwillingness to get involved in politics. Except privately, among intimate friends, he never commented on Athens's politics and her rulers. He said nothing for the record about Pericles and his regime, for or against. He neither supported nor condemned the Peloponnesian War. He did not discuss the excesses of Alcibiades, applaud his victories, or condemn his follies and failures. So far as we know, he had no public comments to make on the fall of Athens and the murderous regime of the Thirty Tyrants. Yet one thing spoke for itself: He chose to remain in Athens during those terrible months. It is true, he refused to have any part in the murder of Leon. But the fact that he then went home and remained there to await retribution instead of fleeing abroad to join the democratic opposition could be held against him. Few understood the nature of his passionate attachment to the streets of the city, even when stained with the blood of its citizens.

Hence it could be said that Socrates was the first man in history, in a formal trial, to fall victim of guilt by association. He had been a friend of both Critias and Alcibiades, and though he denied having taught either of them, he would not repudiate the friendship to satisfy the court. So he was judged guilty. The verdict, considering the number of jurors, was a narrow one. A total of 280 jurors voted for condemnation, 220 for acquittal: a majority of 60. Under Athenian law, the accused was now entitled to propose an alternative to the death sentence demanded by the prosecuting trio. It was universally expected, at any rate by those who did not know him well, that Socrates would propose his banishment. But this was unacceptable to him for two reasons. First, it meant leaving Athens. This, as he saw it, was a greater punishment than death. Second, to have made an alternative punishment proposal acceptable to the court—as banishment certainly would have been— seemed to Socrates to admit the justice of the verdict and the whole process of prosecuting him in the first place.

Instead, and doubtless against the advice of his friends—if he consulted them—Socrates made a defiant counterproposal. It had two attractions for him. First, it maintained his position that his philosophical ministrations to Athenian citizens, including the young, were a positive benefit to his native city and should be rewarded, not punished. Second, this audacious response was a piece of delicious irony and could be couched in his habitual quasicomic tone. He proposed that, in view of the good he had done to Athens by his work, he should be treated like one of the victors in the Olympic Games or like certain generals, admirals, and statesmen who had rendered exceptional services to the city, and awarded his meals at the celebratory table in the Prytaneum—this rare privilege to be conferred on him for life.

This proposal was intended to shock, and did, but

chiefly his own supporters. It appeared to show contempt for the court and its verdict. In response to their frantic signals, Socrates then changed tack. He made a counter-proposal that was punitive. He said he would pay a fine, of one *mina*, which was all he possessed. He added that he was sure his friends would stand surety for a larger fine, if the court felt this appropriate, and put forward a figure of 30 minas. This figure, which he seems to have produced from the top of his head, was not negligible. One *mina*, he knew, would buy a well-produced copy of a play, a history or a poem by Homer at one of the new manuscript shops in the marketplace. Thirty *minas* would constitute an ad-equate dowry for a middle-class bride. But such a fine would not normally be considered a serious alternative to a death sentence, and the proposal of a *mina* fine would have seemed an insult, like his ironic demand to have a seat at the public table in perpetuity.

Socrates made a grievous misjudgment in treating this part of his trial with what most would have seen as levity, if not impudence. This error was reflected in the voting figures for his sentence. Eighty of the jury switched their votes from Socrates to his accusers, and he was con-demned to death by a hugely increased majority—360 to 140. If Socrates was disturbed by this swing of Athenian opinion against him, he gave no overt sign of it. His behavior throughout the long day of his trial was composed and relaxed. He behaved as a man of his calling should do and took his reverses philosophically. He then had plenty of time to reflect upon his wisdom or lack of it. According to Athenian customary law, a sentence of death had to be carried out the day after it was pronounced. On the other hand, no execution was permitted during a period of ceremonial purity. One of these had begun the day before the trial to mark the annual commemoration of the deliverance of Athens by Theseus, the pious myth being renewed by the dispatch of a sanctified boat to the shrine of Apollo on Delos. Until it returned, the state of purity remained, and the execution was postponed.

Socrates' rich friend Crito proposed to the court that Socrates remain at liberty, under his surety, until the boat got back. But the court refused. He was instead put into the city jail and fettered at night to prevent escape. This indignity inflicted on an old man of seventy who had served Athens honorably in her wars and was in no sense a threat to the public peace, strikes us as cruel. But these were cruel times. The defeat in war, the Spartan occupation, the terror imposed by the Thirty, and the bout of civil war that got rid of them had been profoundly demoralizing for a normally self-confident and easygoing city. Locking up their most famous philosopher in chains, as a prelude to his execution was evidence of a psychological crisis that had enveloped the once-proud city in hatred, guilt, and vengefulness. In fairness, one has to remember that most Athenian families had suffered violence within the last three or four years and were still lamenting a murdered father, brother, or son. The atmosphere was raw, bitter, and brutal, and only in this implacable moral climate was it possible for the capital of the civilized world to commit what Aristotle was to call its "crime against philosophy."

However, the official decision to keep Socrates under duress and chained at night was mitigated by allowing him unlimited visitors by day. Many from home and abroad took advantage of the opportunity to see and talk to the famous seer, now in the shadow of death. Contrary winds delayed the sacred boat for a month, and Socrates spent it in the way that gave him most delight—questioning and speaking to those he respected and loved about the things that mattered: virtue, wisdom, the soul, and death.

He did other things too. He wrote poetry. He composed a paean, or hymn of praise, to Apollo. He turned some of Aesop's fables into verse. Socrates explained why he made these efforts in a field that had always been foreign to him. He said he had a regular dream in which he appeared to be commanded to "practice music." He had always interpreted this to mean "do philosophy," for the search for wisdom is the finest music. But the dream had come again, and since he could not practice his kind of philosophy in prison, he felt that perhaps his dream was now to be taken in a more literal sense: making the music of words.

In fact, as all who have read Plato's account of Socrates' last days know, it was not impossible to philosophize in prison. Quite the contrary. Socrates' thinking and his powers of expressing it reached their highest pitch during his prison days. It was as though the physical restraints on his body, by the kind of paradox he loved, released his mind and soul into a freedom he had never known before. He thought more clearly and luminously than ever, and his expressions took on a kind of beauty that Plato, happily, had the genius to convey. We must not suppose we can enjoy the full glory of the results, at any rate in translation. Ancient Greek is a magical language, both written and spoken. Like ancient Hebrew, it has undertones and overtones, echoes and melodies of its own, which point and counterpoint the strange gifts of the extraordinary peoples who spoke them. Ultimately all that is most worthwhile in the Western civilization we cherish can be traced back to Greek and Hebrew words and their humming, resonating meanings. Socrates, in his last days, gave full expression to the specifically Greek component in this intellectual magic. The Greek he spoke was prose and poetry at the same time. And more: It was as though philosophy, so long nurtured in the Greek breast, had found its authentic voice for the first time and was speaking aloud for all future generations to hear.

Socrates in prison, about to die for the right to express his opinions, is an image of philosophy for all time. It caught Plato's imagination and brought forth all his powers. Thanks to those powers, it caught the imagination of all those since who have cared about the importance and penetration of thought. This overwhelmingly potent visual image of the thinking, righteous man on the eve of death, became the archetype of philosophy in its human incarnation. All future philosophers were, in a sense, forced to compete with this image and submit to it.

There was a prelude to the last act of Socrates' life, related in a dialogue with Crito. He was by now Socrates' most constant and closest friend, and he came to see him in prison to propose a means of escape. It would not be difficult, and he would finance it. Socrates, he said, owed it to his children to adopt the plan. The old man, as we might expect, rejected it, though as we would also expect, courteously and patiently. (It is one of the most agreeable aspects of studying Socrates that we are never aware of any sharpness or irritability, of dogmatic emphasis, let alone exasperation, in his tone of voice. His conversational manners are always impeccable.) He took the opportunity to explain the true relationship between philosophy and the law.

Socrates had always felt bound to fulfill his mission. It was his duty to God, as well as his delight and the meaning of his entire existence. Somehow, that mission had come in conflict with the law—as perceived by some—and he had been prosecuted. He had failed in his defense to resolve this conflict and clear up what must be a misunderstanding. So he had been sentenced to death. It was better to die over and over again than to neglect duty, which was obviously and incontrovertibly wrong. Obedience to God came before any law, however righteous. But that was not to defy law, merely to accept the consequences, even death, of obeying a higher law. That led to the second point. Socrates had been born, had been brought up and had lived all his life under Athenian law. He had chosen to do so, over and over again. He regarded Athens as the best place on earth to live, and it had always provided him with the perfect setting for his mission in life. He loved its people, with all their faults, its streets and their trades, its public places. Its government was always imperfect, often grievously remiss, and sometimes monstrous. But it was his city, which he had fought for, and to which he belonged inextricably. Everyone, even or especially philosophers, had to accept the rule of law of the place where they lived. In his case, this rule had come into conflict with his higher calling. The result was a sentence of death. He thought his conviction was mistaken and his sentence unjust. But to seek to evade it by bribery and corruption would be an even greater wrong, an unarguable and incontrovertible injustice that he could never perpetrate. If, as he believed, he was the victim of injustice, how could this be put right by committing an even greater injustice, greater in that he knew it to be unjust? The governing principle of his life was that a wrong could never justify a further wrong in response. Far better to submit to injustice, in the hope and confident expectation that, in time, men and women would come to see it so, and cherish his memory for his fortitude in accepting it.

The *Crito* dialogue concerns the rule of law and its paramountcy. The final dialogue, *Phaedo*, named after one of Socrates' closest followers, who was with him in his last hours, concerns death and the immortal soul. It is Plato's finest work and calls forth all the resources of Socrates' sinuous intellect and the subtlety and beauty of the ancient Greek language. It begins soon after dawn, with the exit of Xanthippe and her child-in-arms, Socrates' third son, who had both evidently spent the night in the prison. His mother apart, Plato was not much interested in women as persons (as opposed to ideas), and therefore we are not told about Xanthippe's thoughts on Socrates' predicament or any advice she gave him. He evidently loved her, to which the young child bore witness, and she him. His leaving her undefended and unprovided for was part of the price he paid for abiding by his principles. But then, as he doubtless consoled himself, he had many devoted friends, some of whose means were ample. It is fruitless to speculate. Socrates is released from his night irons, and as he stirs back into life, muscles wearied by the shackles, he reflects upon how closely the pleasure of release is related, indeed caused by the pain of restriction, an instance of the eternal opposites that punctuate and furnish our lives, giving them movement and variety and richness.

The men—they are a group of close followers and admirers, some from abroad—then get down to the final matters that dominate Socrates' last hours: death and what follows, or rather the death and disappearance of the body and the survival of the soul in a place prepared for it. It is Socrates' great merit as a philosopher that he always concentrates on what matters most to us. Of course it is interesting to know what set the universe in motion, if anything did, and what follows from Einstein's general theory of relativity, and whether there is such a thing as antimatter, and other objects of speculation and experimental inquiry. These or similar questions interested the Greeks in 399 B.C. as they interest us today. But what really mattered then and matters now is the one inescapable fact of human existence: death, and what follows it. Despite all the efforts of doctors and scientists, psychologists, poets, painters, musicians, and other imaginative creators of genius, death remains as great a mystery to us now as it did to Socrates' contemporaries 2,500 years ago. In knowledge of death we have not advanced one centimeter in all that time. Our perception of life to come, if there is any, is no more vivid. If anything, cloudier. But thanks to Socrates—and to Plato for recording him—we have at least learned, if we choose, to approach death and an unknown future with decorum, courage, and honor.

Socrates told those listening to him that the true philosopher has no fear of death or desire to resist it, because he is willing to die as an affirmation of the principles by which he has striven to live. The philosopher, by whom he meant all those anxious to live and do wisely, knows that after death, the soul of the just man will be in the care of a god who values justice above all things and therefore will ensure that the still living soul of the dead man will be comforted and made secure. Death, then, is not to be feared but to be welcomed as the natural end to our life on earth and the beginning of something infinitely more glorious.

There follows an argumentative justification of Socrates' firm belief that the soul is indeed immortal and survives when the body rots away. This passage is spoiled by Plato's irritating insistence on dragging into it and foisting on a reluctant (we assume) Socrates his theory of forms. But this is a detail that does not matter, for Socrates' confidence in the survival of the soul and in the emotional, intellectual, and spiritual richness that awaits the souls of the just is so calm, serene, pure, and magisterial as to carry all before it. Socrates does not necessarily remove all doubts in the mind of the skeptic about the soul's immortality and the afterlife. What he does do, however, is convince us of his own belief in both and of the steadfastness with which he approaches his own departure into the unknown.

The supreme lesson of Socrates' life, it seems to me, is that doing justice according to the best of your knowledge gives you a degree of courage that no inbred or trained valor could possibly equal. If there was one particular virtue Socrates possessed, it was courage, shown in all kinds of circumstances, from the battlefield to the courtroom, and now in his last hours under sentence of death. Thanks to his incisive arguments in favor of the immortal soul and the life waiting for it after the body departed—arguments that expressed his own total inner conviction—Socrates' own spirits rose and rose during his last hours, until by the time death was imminent, they overflowed in a great, steady, copious fountain of optimism and expectation. He embraced death not as a punishment but as a reward. It culminated, crowned, beatified, and made luminous his entire life.

As dusk fell, the discussion came to its natural end, and the jailer arrived to announce that Socrates must now take poison. It was an axiom of the Athenian democracy that the laws, being freely voted, must be freely complied with by citizens, even and especially the punishment of death, which must be administered by the person condemned, who was required to swallow poison. This was composed of hemlock, though Plato does not explicitly say so, and it may have been a mixture more certain to produce death quickly, surely, and painlessly than a simple distillation of the noxious plant. The jailer could not help but tell those present that Socrates was the noblest, the gentlest, and the bravest man he had ever had in his custody, and his obvious distress at the work he had to do was, perhaps, the most striking tribute to the lovable nature of the seer, to anyone fortunate enough to know him well.

Before taking the poison, Socrates had a bath and again said good-bye to his children and the women of his family: "He talked to them in Crito's presence," says Plato, "and gave them directions about his last wishes." Then he rejoined his friends, and later a man came in with the poison in a cup. Socrates said, "Well, my friend, you are accustomed to these things—what do I do?" "Just drink it, Sir, and then walk about until you feel your legs becoming heavy. Then lie down, and the poison will do its work." He handed the cup to Socrates, who received it cheerfully, without any trembling or change of color or expression. He asked if he might perform a libation (an offering to the gods), but the man said the cup contained only enough for its purpose. "Well," said Socrates, "I can still pray that my departure from this world will be beneficent. So I do pray, and I hope my prayer will be granted." With these words he drank the cup, in one long swallow, quite calmly, and with no sign of repugnance.

At this point, his friends, who had been anxious to show self-restraint, began to weep. Crito, to compose himself, left the room. Apollodorus, already weeping, erupted in a spasm of convulsive tears, which set everyone else going, and brought a rebuke from Socrates himself: "What a way for men to behave! I sent away my womenfolk to prevent this kind of scene. I planned to die in a reverent silence, and now your tears are forcing me to joke! Pray, be calm, and brave." So it was, over two millennia later, when W. E. Gladstone, the great Liberal statesman, announced to his fourth and last cabinet, in 1894, that he was resigning as prime minister and ending his political career of over sixty years. There were tears on all sides, and Gladstone, dry-eyed and sardonic, called it "my blubbering cabinet." Socrates made no reference to "my blubbering death scene." Instead, he walked about for a while, until he said, "I shall lie down. My legs are heavy." He lay on his back, as the poison bearer recommended. The man then examined his feet and legs, then pinched one foot hard and asked if he felt it. Socrates said no. The man then pinched his legs and moved to the center of his body, finding all cold and numb. He told those watching, "When the numbness reaches his heart, Socrates will be no more."

Suddenly, however, the old man drew back the covers he had placed over his face and said clearly, "Crito, we ought to offer a cock to Asclepius. Do so, and don't forget." These were his last words. Some early Christian writers used to cite them as evidence of Socrates' incorrigible paganism: thinking of a childish sacrifice to the god of healing on his deathbed. In fact it was more a sign of Socrates' love of joking and irony. He was anxious to thank God for a safe transit from fretful life into easeful death, and "a cock for Asclepius" was his droll way of putting it. So he passed away with a smile.

VII

Socrates and
Philosophy Personified

In terms of his influence, Socrates was the most important of all philosophers. He supplied some of the basic apparatus of the human mind, especially in the way men and women approach moral choices and make them, and in the consequences that flow from them in this world and the next.

Socrates did not exactly abolish the fantastic polytheism of ancient Greek paganism, with its humanlike gods and goddesses and its godlike heroes apotheosized into deities and all their fictionalized and poetic feuds, favoritism, magic, miracles, and interventions. This pantheon was fading fast even in his lifetime, and Socrates, always tender toward the superstitions of others, did not assault it frontally. What he did was to concentrate on making more substantial the presence of an overriding divine force, a God who permeated all things and ordained the universe. This dramatic simplification made it possible for him to construct a system of ethics that was direct, plausible, workable, and satisfying.

Socrates did this by drawing an absolute distinction between the body and the soul. The body was the source of desires, appetites, gratifications, and glory. It represented the animal nature of man, his physical being and his ambitions and pleasures, both legitimate and harmful. Without this body, humans were nothing and could do nothing; they needed the body to be significant, creative, and purposeful. The body was a problem and burden, however, because of the sheer power of its desires and the destruction involved in gratifying them. But the body was balanced by the soul, which represented the principle of virtue and wisdom; the two were intimately connected and in some respects indistinguishable. The body was the outward form; the soul was the inward personality of the human being. The more the appetites of the body were controlled and restrained, the more the soul prospered and flourished, and the personality of the human became benevolent, useful, and at ease with himself and the world. The body pursued pleasure, hoping to find happiness. But happiness was to be found, in this life, only by allowing the soul to direct the body in the path of virtue and wisdom. The body came to an end with death, and rotted away, taking its problems and appetites away too. The soul survived, and if guided in this life by virtue and wisdom, found itself prepared to be united with God and with other well-nurtured souls in an immortal existence of content.

The permeation of Greek thought by Socrates' notions of life and death, body and soul, which operated through the writings of Plato and Aristotle and others, and which became increasingly perceptible within two or three generations of his departure, was hugely assisted by the story of his trial and self-execution and his superb composure on the threshold of eternity. Socrates became not only the archetypal philosopher and source of ethical wisdom, but the living paradigm of a good man and the perfect example of how the body-soul relationship ought to operate.

Hence when in the first century A.D. St. Paul came to preach the teachings of Jesus Christ to the Greek-speaking world of the Gentiles, he found an audience already prepared, in certain important respects, for his message. It was the combination of Jesus' inspired Hebrew message of charity, selflessness, acceptance of suffering, and willing sacrifice with the clear Socratic vision of the soul's triumph and the eternal life awaiting it that gave the Christianity which sprang from St. Paul's teaching of the Gospels its astonishing power and ubiquity and enabled it to flourish in persecution and martyrdom. The figure of

Socrates also emerged unscathed and ennobled from his trial, conviction, and approaching death. St. Paul wrote, "The Greeks ask for a reason, the Jews look for a sign." Socrates, thanks to Plato's writings, supplied the reason, while Jesus of Nazareth and his resurrection produced the sign.

It is not profitable to pursue the connection between Socratic thought and Christianity beyond this general point. Socrates was not a Christian precursor, and though, like Jesus, he had a mission, the two endeavors had little in common. "I am the way, the truth and the life": this was a majestic claim, which only the consciousness of divinity could possibly justify. It was not a prospectus Socrates could ever conceivably have put forward. His one reiterated insistence was that he knew nothing. What he did feel he could do, and what was the essence of his ministry, was to help ordinary humans to think a little more clearly and coherently about what constituted good behavior, worthy of humanity at its best. The success with which he did this, worked out over numerous generations, gave clarity and power to the Greek world's reception of Christianity and so made it more fruitful. That in itself was an enormous achievement, beside which the work of Plato and Aristotle, important though they were in the establishment of

Christendom and so of the Western world that succeeded it, were peripheral contributions.

The second key way in which Socrates furnished or refurnished the mind permanently was in insisting that morality was absolute, not relative. All societies, from the most primitive to the most sophisticated, have an inherent, weakening tendency to slip into moral relativism. Greek society as he found it was a crumbling and festering mass of morally relative practices and pseudo-idealistic propositions to justify them. The body of Greek polytheism sweated moral relativism at every pore. It would be hard to find a clear moral absolute in the whole of Homer, and dramatists like Sophocles and Euripides tell approvingly of deals with the gods that subvert the notion of regular moral conduct. Socrates' great gift to society was that he brought morals from the shifty atmosphere of quasidivine bargains, frauds, and compromises into the blazing daylight of ordinary honorable transactions between men and women striving to be honest. To Socrates, morality was absolute or it was nothing. If an act was unjust, it was always and everywhere so and must never be done. Whatever the provocation, a man or woman must never act unjustly. A simple tradesman doing his business in the Agora at Athens, a statesman speaking to the Assembly on issues of peace or war, a general or admiral conducting an army or a galley fleet, or a teacher instructing the young were all subject to the same inexorable moral laws.

Socrates rejected retaliation, however great the offense in the first place, as contrary to justice because it involved inflicting a wrong. The principle—never retaliate, never inflict wrong in any circumstances—applied equally to city-states, however powerful, and private individuals, however humble. Socrates drew no distinction between public and private morality, a point never before made or even considered in the history of Greek ethics—if ethics could be said to have had a history before his time. It might be said that Socrates, in subjecting all actors on the human stage to the same rules, democratized ethics in the same way, though by a different process of reasoning, that the ancient Hebrews made all humans equal in subjection to an omnipotent and universal Yahweh and so produced what Philo of Alexandria, a seer who owed almost as much to Socrates as to Moses, called a democratic theocracy.

Socrates had a favorable opinion of men and women because he saw clearly that they were capable of the highest moral heroism. Their outward appearance was of no lasting significance. Beauty faded with age, and clothes could do little for a man or woman to enhance or detract from what nature had provided. He had no shoes and precious little in the way of garments, and God had made him an ugly man. On the other hand, he was no uglier at seventy than he had been at twenty: a little more bandy-legged, perhaps, and with a paunch. He had no time for Zeuxis, the fashionable painter who had his name embroidered on his cloak in gold letters. What was that supposed to prove? On the other hand, human beings, though not worth adorning, were infinitely worth study. Socrates was fascinated throughout his life by the variety, peculiarities, cussedness, and sheer individualism of human beings. They posed problems he delighted in solving and offered perspectives on the human condition that kept him in constant fascination as he bustled and dawdled about the streets of Athens, sampling its human wares. Asked why he had married such a difficult woman as Xanthippe, he replied that it was precisely her singularities, not to say her angularities, that made her attractive. She was a problem to be solved on which he could exercise his skills, like a horse trainer, he added, confronted by a testing but remarkable animal. Socrates was interested in ideas and concepts, and they form the starting point of all the dialogues in which Plato shows him participating. But the dialogues live and have meaning only in their humanity, only because they deal with real individuals. For Socrates, ideas existed to serve and illuminate people, not the other way around. Here was the big distinction between him and Plato. To Socrates, philosophy had no meaning or relevance unless it concerned itself with men and women. It is worth repeating, and emphasizing, Cicero's summary of Socrates' work: "He was the first to call philosophy down from the sky and establish her in the towns, and bring her into homes, and force her to investigate the life of men and women, ethical conduct, good and evil."

Hence Socrates was ill at ease when by himself. He could not exercise his philosophy as a solitary. He needed people. He needed a city. Above all, he needed Athens. He had to have its human content, of all ages and classes and callings, to call upon and buttonhole, to question and sift, to stir up and provoke. It was as if he were a master chef preparing a celebratory feast of humanity. The Athenians were his prime ingredient, to which by his "examining" he added spice and flavor, substance and body, balance and variety, until he had produced a banquet of the mind and spirit that has given the world nourishment ever since.

Happy among people, Socrates did not seek to turn them into pupils, let alone students. He was not a teacher, a don, an academic. There was nothing professorial about him. He had no oeuvre. As Cicero said, "He did not write so much as a single letter." There was no body of Socratic doctrine. He spurned a classroom. The streets and marketplace of Athens were his habitat. Unlike Plato and Aristotle, he founded no Academy or Lyceum. The university, with its masters and students, its lectures and tutorials, its degrees and libraries and publishing houses, was nothing to do with him. He was part of the life of the city—a thinking part, to be sure, a talking and debating part, but no more separated from its throbbing, bustling activity than the fishmonger or the money changer or the cobbler, its ranting politician, its indigent poet, or its wily lawyer. He was at home in the city, a stranger on campus. He knew that as soon as philosophy separated itself from the life of the people, it began to lose its vitality and was heading in the wrong direction. An academic philosophy was not an activity to which he had anything of value to contribute or in which he wished to participate. The notion of philosophy existing only in academic isolation from the rest of the world would have horrified him and probably would have produced ribald laughter, too. "That," one can hear him saying, "is the death of any philosophy I can recognize."

For Socrates saw and practiced philosophy not as an academic but as a human activity. It was about real men and women facing actual ethical choices between right and wrong, good and evil. Hence a philosophical leader had to be more than a thinker, much more. He had to be a good man, for whom the quest for virtue was not an abstract idea but a practical business of daily living. He had to be brave in facing up to choices and living with their consequences. Philosophy, in the last resort, was a form of heroism, and those who practiced it had to possess the courage to sacrifice everything, including life itself, in pursuing excellence of mind. That is what Socrates himself did. And that is why we honor him and salute him as philosophy personified.

FURTHER READING

The handiest collection of texts that form the primary sources for Socrates' life is *On Socrates* in the Collector's Library (London, 2004), with an introduction by Tom Griffith. This gives the seven most important texts of Plato (*Lysis, Laches, Charmides, Symposium, Apology, Crito,* and *Phaedo*) the text of *Clouds* by Aristophanes, and Xenophon's *Symposium*. Moreover, it slips easily into the pocket. A more extensive collection of texts is in *Socrates: A Source Book*, compiled by John Ferguson (London, for the Open University, 1970), which gives much more of Plato, Xenophon's *Memoirs of Socrates*, Diogenes Laertius, a good deal of Aristotle, and extracts dealing with Socrates from Cicero and many other Latin secular writers, Plutarch and other Greek writers, and Christian writers on Socrates. Other editions of texts I have found useful include the Penguin *Last Days of Socrates* (*Euthyphro, Apology, Crito, Phaedo*), edited by Harold Tarrent, and the Penguin *Republic*, translated by Desmond Lee with an introduction by Melissa Lane (London, 1987).

Two good, short biographies of Socrates are by A. E. Taylor (London, 1932) and C. C. W. Taylor (Oxford, 1998). *Plato,* by R. M. Hare (Oxford, 1982), is also recommended. The key book on Socrates is by Gregory Vlastos, *Socrates: Ironist and Moral Philosopher* (Cambridge, 1997). Also useful are the *Cambridge Companion to Plato,* edited by Richard Krant (Cambridge, 1992); Jonathan Barnes, *Early Greek Philosophy* (London, 2001); Karl Popper, *The Open Society and Its Enemies,* vol. 1, *The Spell of Plato* (London, 2005); and Nickolas Pappas, *Plato and the Republic* (London, 1996). For art, architecture, and sculpture, I have used Martin Robertson, *A History of Greek Art,* 2 vols. (Cambridge, 1975); K. Papaioannou, *The Art of Greece* (New York, 1989); and J. J. Pollitt, *Art and Experience in Classical Greece* (Cambridge, 1972). For general background, see the *Oxford Classical Dictionary,* edited by N. G. L. Hammond and H. H. Scullard (Oxford, 1973) and the *Oxford Companion to Classical Literature,* edited by M. C. Howatson (Oxford, 1993).

INDEX

Index

Index

Index

Index

moral absolutism of, 113–16, 119–21, 189–90

retaliation rejected in, 114–21, 134, 148, 190

slavery and, 132–34

for women, 121, 126–32

Keynes, John Maynard, 105

Knights (Aristophanes), 64

Laches (Plato), 24, 88–90, 108

Laws (Plato), 132

Leibniz, Gottfried Wilhelm von, 109

Leonidas, 22

Leon of Salamis, 146, 165

Longford, Frank, 32

lyre, 53, 54–55, 75

Lysander, 145

Lysias, 123–24

Lysistrata (Aristophanes), 64

Macaulay, Thomas Babington, 85

maenads, 58

Marathon, Battle of, 21–22, 60

mathematics, 50–51, 53, 78

Medea (Euripides), 116–17

Megacles, 151

Meletus, 149–50, 160

Memoirs (Xenophon), 9

Meno (Plato), 149

Miltiades, 22, 99

Moore, Henry, 25

Moore, Thomas, 32

moral education, 5–8, 53, 108, 112

More, Thomas, 39

Munich Gallery of Antique Art, 54

music, 6, 21, 52–55, 58, 63, 97, 129, 169–70

musical ethics, 53, 56

musical instruments, 53, 54–55, 56, 63, 75

Myrto, 32

Mytilene, 117–19

Nicias, 89–90, 107–8, 141–43, 152

Nietzsche, Friedrich, 96

Olympic games, 19–21, 166

Open Society and Its Enemies, The (Popper), 94–95

Oracle of Delphi, 83, 161–62

paeans, 55–56, 169

Panhellenic games, 19–21

Parmenides, 76–77

Parrhasius, 25

Index

Index

Index

Index

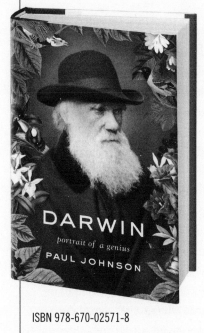

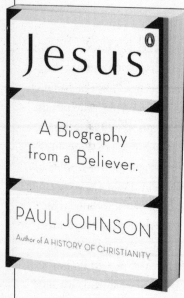

Churchill

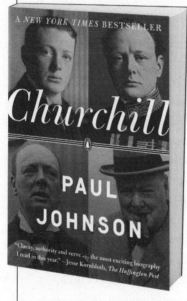

Winston Churchill's hold on contemporary readers has never slackened, and this exploration of his life casts new light on one of history's most intriguing figures. Johnson illuminates the various phases of Churchill's career— from his adventures as a young cavalry officer in the service of the empire to his role as an elder statesman prophesying the advent of the Cold War—and shows how Churchill's immense adaptability and innate pugnacity made him a formidable leader for the better part of a century.

PENGUIN BOOKS

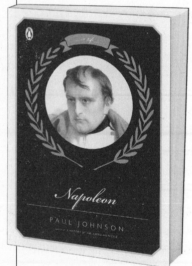